PSALMS
FOR
TRIALS

PSALMS FOR TRIALS

MEDITATIONS ON

PRAYING THE PSALMS

Lindsey Tollefson

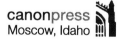

canonpress
Moscow, Idaho

Published by Canon Press
P.O. Box 8729, Moscow, Idaho 83843
800.488.2034 | www.canonpress.com

Library of Congress Cataloging-in-Publication Data
Tollefson, Lindsey, author.
The Psalms for us : meditations on the Psalms / Lindsey Tollefson.
Moscow : Canon Press, 2018. | Includes bibliographical
   references and index.
LCCN 2018024509 | ISBN 9781947644038 (pbk. : alk. paper)
Bible. Psalms—Commentaries.
Classification: LCC BS1430.53 .T65 2018 | DDC 223/.206--dc23
LC record available at https://lccn.loc.gov/2018024509

18 19 20 21 22 23 24 25   9 8 7 6 5 4 3 2 1

To Jon,
My co-heir in this gracious gift of life.

CONTENTS

PART II

PRAISING WITH THE PSALMS

PART III

PREACHING THE PSALMS TO YOURSELF

FOREWORD

THERE ARE A FEW THINGS THAT THE WORLD can never get too much of, and one of those things is women who fear the Lord, are saturated in His Word, and practice the things they find there. We simply cannot have too much of this: there is no such thing as an overdose of practical spirituality. The more women who seek to apply Scripture to their lives, the better. The more women who habitually look for ways to conform their thoughts to the Word of God, for ways to let the Word of God shape their behavior as well as their emotions, the better. It isn't the kind of thing that you can overdo—but it is actually the kind of thing that many Christians have never even *tried* to do.

We long with the prophet Habakkuk for the day when "The earth will be filled with the knowledge of the glory of the LORD, as the waters cover the sea" (2:14).

This glory begins in the lives of normal believers—people who let their own lives be washed over in the knowledge of the glory of the Lord. Let it cover you completely. Let it cover your life. Your thought life. Your children's lives. The world was made for this glory, and it all starts with normal obedience, normal faithfulness, and normal listening to what the Word of the Lord is telling us.

Lindsey offers us here just this kind of normal obedience. Look to the Word, look to your life, apply what you learned, repeat it forever. Like a bucket brigade bringing the knowledge of the glory of the Lord to the earth, may the Lord raise up many women who will take their place in this line, encouraging one another with Psalms and hymns and spiritual songs as we give our strength to the kingdom.

RACHEL JANKOVIC
July 2018

PREFACE

EVERYTHING CHANGED THE SUMMER THAT I turned fourteen. We had been living for the previous three years in Cambridge, England where there was always a heavy cloud cover and the vegetation was lush. A few months after my father finished school, he accepted a teaching position in Idaho and our family of ten drove across the United States for the first time. As we came to the last leg of our journey, we drove from the mountains in northern Idaho into the Palouse: a land of rolling hills and farms, with few trees. The sky felt uncomfortably huge, and the space empty. When we arrived it was early August and the fields were gold and dry. Dust clouds formed on the dirt roads surrounding our new house. I took one step out of the van and a sea of brown grasshoppers fled. *Where are we?* I thought, *What is this desert?* The contrast of moving from England to Idaho was stark, but the irony was strong in our story. What had literally looked like a lush garden had been something of a spiritual desert for us, and what looked at the beginning like a wilderness was going to become a garden of life for our family.

A few weeks after we moved to Idaho we attended a Psalm Sing in the living room of a doctor's home. We found a wonderful church to attend, and every month they met to sing psalms together. The first time we attended, I sat on the stairs that overlooked a living room which held a sea of strangers. Through a nearby window I could see the sunset reflecting pink on the mountain. The crowd below belted out Psalm 42: "As the hart, about to falter, in its trembling agony, longs for flowing streams of water, so, Oh God, I long for Thee." I had been learning the Psalms since I was a small child, but I had not realized how much I needed them to guide me through my life until I began to sing them regularly.

The transition to Idaho was hard. The move took several months to complete, and I changed from homeschooling to attending private school, which meant that my laziness in my previous studies was showing itself. I was very behind the rest of the class, and I was scrambling to catch up. I joined the volleyball team to try to make some friends, but I soon found that I was terrible at it, and I spent every game on the bench. I was insecure and awkward and confused. Psalm 42 stuck to my bones, and at many times I found myself overwhelmed and humiliated by my own inabilities, not knowing what to pray for, whispering those words: "As the hart...so my soul longs for You." When everything I was trying to do was failing, when all my inabilities were showing themselves strongly, these were sometimes the only words that made sense. I knew that even though my childish struggles were overwhelming to me, in God was found the security that I needed and in Him was the wisdom that I lacked.

Twenty years have passed since I first landed in Idaho, and my love for the Psalms has continued to grow. My trials and challenges have become more difficult than learning high school Latin. God has led me through many hardships that are common: financial difficulties, miscarriage, illness, complications in pregnancy, moving, job loss, loneliness, learning contentment, learning to be a mother, and wrestling with my own pride and selfishness. Through all these I have looked to the Psalms to shape my prayers and my thoughts. I am not writing to you as someone who has a perfectly peaceful life, but rather as someone who needs the Psalms every day to keep me afloat. Many of the examples that I offer in this book are from my own experience. I am a wife and a mother, and I look for ways the Psalms can encourage me in my current calling. But I encourage you to think of how the Psalms can meet you in your current calling. Are you jolting through the teenage years, learning what it means to be an adult? Are you struggling with chronic illness? Are you climbing the mountain of higher education? Are you trying to start a school or a church? Are you faithfully working a job that is not what you dreamed of? Are you adjusting to the quietness of empty nesting? My hope with this book is to show you how the Psalms can shape your prayers and thoughts as you walk through the common challenges of life. My hope is that as you read the Psalms you will start to see God as a person in your life who is working through and in all the details. I hope you will begin to talk to Him constantly. I challenge you, after reading each section in this book, to find words in the Psalms for your prayers, as well as encouragement and perseverance in your particular situation. I hope that as you start praying the Psalms, you will feel His presence in all the things that you do, and you will feel His guidance both through storms and long periods of waiting. I hope that you will see God as your life and breath instead of as your religion.

The book of Psalms is unique, because it is neither history nor exhortation, and unlike Proverbs and Ecclesiastes, it is not addressed to a person in order to teach wisdom. Psalms is a song book, most of it originally set to music, but it is also a prayer book, with the words usually addressed to the Lord. Seventy-three of the Psalms are written by King David, twelve by Asaph who was a songwriter for David, twelve by the Levites who were working under David, two by King Solomon, one each by the songwriters Heman and Ethan, and one by Moses. They were written to teach the people of God how to praise Him and how to plead with Him. Although the

Psalms were written thousands of years ago, their words are still helpful for us in our prayers, in our worship, and in our trials.

We can learn much theology from the Psalms, especially about what kind of person God is. We can learn how to talk to Him, and we can learn how He responds. We can learn what He thinks is important. We can learn what it looks like to pray without ceasing. The Psalms address every area of our hearts: sin, confession, pain, loss, joy, shame, gratitude, fear, and much more. We can come to a better understanding of our relationship with God. We can see how He relates to us and how much He loves us. Timothy Keller puts it this way: "Psalms anticipate and train you for every possible spiritual, social, and emotional condition—they show you what the dangers are, what you should keep in mind, what your attitude should be, how to talk to God about it, and how to get from God the help you need."*

When you begin to read the Psalms, some of them may seem distant, especially the later psalms that were written while Israel was in captivity in Babylon. They talk about exile and longing for the temple, specific situations that many of us do not quite relate to. But our God is both infinite and specific. His words transcend time. The more you learn the Psalms, the more you find the words apply to your own life, even though the original context is vastly different. The Spirit has

* Timothy Keller, *The Songs of Jesus: A Year of Daily Devotions in the Psalms* (New York: Viking, 2015), viii.

not changed since the time of David, and the words
He gave King David while he hid from his father-in-law
Saul in the caves are the same words He will use to comfort you when you are in the grip of fear. God is writing
a cosmic story, but at the same time He is writing each
specific day. Do not let the contextual distance of the
Psalms prevent you from clinging to them as your own
prayers and your own promises. The context of God's
Word is helpful and necessary for understanding the
meaning, but God is not bound by context. He finds
us where we are and gives us the same words that He
gave David.

One of the most fascinating mysteries of the Psalms is
that many describe Christ and His suffering, while at the
same time describing David and his suffering. Now that
we are in Christ, the words of the Psalms can also comfort us in our sufferings. Bonhoeffer explains it this way,

> How is it possible for a man and Jesus Christ to
> pray the Psalter together? It is the incarnate Son of
> God, who has borne every human weakness in his
> own flesh, and who here pours out the heart of all
> humanity before God and who stands in our place
> and prays for us. He has known torment and pain,
> guilt and death more deeply than we. Therefore it
> is the prayer of the human nature assumed by him
> which comes before God. It is really our prayer, but
> since he knows us better than we know ourselves
> and since he himself was true man for our sakes,

it is also really his prayer, and it can become our prayer only because it was his prayer.*

When the Lord hung, dying on the cross, He quoted Psalm 22:1, "My God, My God, why have you forsaken Me?" This entire psalm is a description of the crucifixion, yet it was written by David many years before. Jesus claims this prayer as His own, and it does describe the physical experience that Christ had more specifically than any experiences David had, especially in verse 16 where it speaks of hands and feet being pierced. Verses 30–31 speak of future generations seeing God's righteousness, which suggests that David knew he was writing something prophetic.

In his *Expositions on the Book of Psalms*, Augustine of Hippo walks through Psalm 22 in great detail, showing how each verse is talking about Christ. It was on the cross that Christ took on all of our sorrow, and all the sorrow of those who came before His incarnation. He gathers us into Himself, and we are made new in Him becoming the representative of the world as first fruits, which means that His words of sorrow not only brought comfort to Him, but also to us, since we are in Him.

We are all connected through Christ. No one is literally dividing my garments and casting lots for my clothing (verse 18), and as far as I know David did not experience that in a literal sense. But our sufferings bring us to pray

* Dietrich Bonhoeffer, *Psalms: The Prayer Book of the Bible* (Augsburg, MN: Fortress, 1970), 21.

with Christ. He experienced great shame the day He died. Do we experience shame? Did David? Because Christ experienced shame, we are given an example of suffering to help us bear it, and we are given words to pray when we feel shame. Descriptions of Jesus appear throughout the Psalms, and we are connected with Him when we pray through them. You will find as you learn more psalms and as you pray through them that, although the psalm is written for Christ and by David or Moses or Asaph, we are all part of the same body through these prayers. Just as Romans 12:5 says, "So we, being many, are one body in Christ, and individually members one of another."

As you read this book, I encourage you to be reading through the Psalms on your own. The context of each passage will be helpful, and my words do not compare with the powerful words in the Psalms themselves. We will be looking at short passages from 46 different psalms. In each section of this book I offer my own meditations on these passages, but I also challenge you to meditate on how these passages can be used in your own prayers and thoughts. These meditations are short enough that you can easily read one a day to create the habit of using the Psalms in your daily life. Many of these meditations are on similar subjects, but repetition is one of the strengths of the Psalms. We learn by repetition. When David prays to God in the Psalms, he often repeats his plea. One of the great encouragements of the Psalms is to remember who God is and what He has done. Repetition is our tool to help us remember.

The Psalms fall into three broad categories: psalms of prayer, psalms of praise, and psalms of preaching. As we look at psalms of prayer, I will show you how to use the words in the Psalms in your own prayers as you persevere through trials. Using the Psalms in prayer is a powerful exercise that many Christians do not practice. As we look at psalms of praise, I will show you how you can use psalms to express gratitude in your prayers. You cannot praise someone you know nothing about, and the Psalms teach us what God is like. The final section is about psalms of preaching. I do not mean preaching as a pastor would do from a pulpit, although these psalms would be good for that too. I am talking about preaching to yourself. In this section you will learn about the promises that are found in the Psalms and how to affirm these truths to find daily encouragement. When we face struggles in life, we will either grow bitterness or grow faith. The Psalms of preaching teach us how to cultivate our faith.

PART I

PRAYING
with the PSALMS

INTRODUCTION

MANY OF THE PSALMS CONTAIN A COMBINATION
of prayers, praises, and passages of preaching the truth.
In this section we will be focusing on portions of the
psalms that are prayers. I encourage you to start using
quotes from the Psalms as you pray. In 1 Thessalonians
5:17, Paul's exhortation to "pray without ceasing" can
seem a little overwhelming. Praying without ceasing
seems impossible. Obviously we can't pray out loud every second of every day; we have to interact verbally with
other people. But can we pray in our hearts all day, every
day, and in any waking hours of the night? The Psalms
are a perfect guide for us in this. We should pray with
our own words to God, but I have found that my words
often run out. I hear of a friend who has been diagnosed
with cancer and I pray, "Lord, give her the strength to
withstand the treatment, give her the courage not to be
afraid as she spends many days in hospitals and many

days at home in pain. I ask that the side effects of her
treatment would be minimal and that you would heal
her and bring her back to full health." These are good
words, but repeating them constantly "without ceasing"
eventually starts to feel desperate. But if I follow these
words with Psalm 103:2–3, "Bless the LORD, O my soul,
and forget not all His benefits: who forgives all your iniquities, who heals all your diseases," then two things
are happening. First, I am reminding God that He is the
One who heals diseases. I am showing that I believe He
is who He says He is, and that He can heal bodies. Second, instead of lifting up my friend in prayer over and
over again and constantly waiting impatiently for an answer, I am praying the answer. God says yes. He is the
One who heals all diseases: He will heal her. Sometimes
His healing comes by bringing His people to Himself,
and sometimes He gives our earthly bodies more years.
But either way, the psalm gives me the answer to my
prayer as I am praying it. While I continue to plead with
God for her comfort and strength and earthly healing, I
can continue to pray without ceasing because the promises in the Psalms have given my prayer hope.

The Psalms encourage us to tell God what we are feeling. David was a man of great courage and faith, and
he had no lack of emotions. Though God knew what
David was feeling, He wanted David to pour out his
heart. In Psalm 6:6 he says, "All night I make my bed
swim; I drench my couch with tears." This might seem
slightly melodramatic to modern evangelicals, but David

knew the context in which he should pour himself out. He knew when it was time to grab his sling and run unarmored into battle with a giant, and he knew when it was time to express his emotions in prayer.

When life seems so overwhelming, we may not even be sure where to begin our prayers. Sometimes God gives us a disappointing answer, and then what do we say to Him? This is where David's words can meet us and give us great comfort. As we learn psalms, we learn what words to use in our own situations. Maybe you are dealing with a physical illness or trying to raise a difficult child or muddling your way through a tough marriage. Maybe you have been pinching pennies for what feels like forever or you have been praying for an open womb. Maybe you just have a hard job and the basic stress of making it through your daily work leaves you feeling exhausted physically and spiritually. This is why you must learn psalms. They will give you the words to help you pour out your heart to God, and they will give you the hope that He hears and that He cares.

PRAYING THROUGH
A TRIAL

It is good for me that I have been afflicted,
that I may learn Your statutes.
PSALM 119:71

Unless Your law had been my delight,
I would then have perished in my affliction.
PSALM 119:92

You are my hiding place and my shield;
I hope in Your word.
Depart from me, you evildoers,
for I will keep the commandments of my God!
Uphold me according to Your word, that I may live;
and do not let me be ashamed of my hope.
Hold me up, and I shall be safe,
and I shall observe Your statutes continually.
PSALM 119:114–117

Consider my affliction and deliver me,
for I do not forget Your law.
PSALM 119:153

Psalm 119 is famously the longest psalm in the Bible with 176 verses. It is a meditation on the excellence of God's law. The psalmist keeps coming back to this theme: Affliction teaches us that there is no sweeter thing to study and to meditate on than God's law. When we are struggling with affliction, we may quickly be tempted to look to human means for help first. Though seeking the help of a doctor or counselor may be wise, we will totally miss the point of the trial if we are not viewing it as a gift from the hand of God and part of His purpose and plan for us. We can learn so much from Psalm 119 about the blessing of trials.

The first thing the psalmist does is express gratitude. He says that it was good for him to be afflicted, because it brought him to Scripture (v. 71). His hardship brought him to seek after God's law, to cry out to God, to look to God for answers about how to live and how to think. When we see our trials as discipline that is testing us and ultimately refining us, we can see the good that God is doing in them. When we view hardships this way, they change us. Give thanks for the change.

Second, the psalmist says that he would have perished in his affliction if he did not delight in God's law (v. 92). His soul would have been consumed with fear, discontent, and anxiety. He found that the only defense was to study the Word of God. Scripture is like the vitamin C for our soul immune systems. Being in the Word creates a strong defense against enemies. When life gets busy and fast, it is harder for us to find time to be in the Word. But what does the psalmist say? You will die without it!

I am well acquainted with the difficulty of keeping a consistent Bible reading routine through normal life changes, but I encourage you to find a time each day when you can feed your soul, no matter how short of a time it is. Whenever our family has faced a big change, it has been hard to keep up with reading my Bible. When we have moved or had a baby, or even transitioned from the school year to the summer months, my routine is changed, and my well-established habits suffer. I have had to learn to make it the most important thing I do in a day. On average, reading one chapter of the Bible takes less than five minutes. Spend five minutes to nourish your soul, and you will find that your soul is thirsty for more.

The third thing that the psalmist does in his trial is to ask God to uphold him. He calls God his "hiding place" and his "shield" (v. 114). Later he asks for deliverance, but here he asks for protection. The psalmist needed physical protection while he was still in the trial. I ask God often to protect me from bitterness, resentment, anger, impatience, and pride. He can be our hiding place from sin in the same way that He was a physical hiding place for the psalmist. When we are in Him, surrounded by the defense of His law, we are safe.

In verse 153 we see the psalmist's fourth step in dealing with his affliction. He asks God to consider him. He argues that he has kept God's law and delighted in God, and now he wants God to notice. He wants God to respond and deliver him. This reminds me of when my children are unhappy with a decision we have made. We tell them to eat their dinner, and after a few bites they ask, "How many more?" They are asking us to remember them, to consider the obedience they have shown, and to revoke the decision. They want to be done with the affliction of eating salad. The psalmist believes that God is the kind of Father who responds to appeal. Even before God became man and lived in the sinful world, the psalmist knew that God was merciful and understanding. How much more can we pray for God to consider us? Christ has become man; He knows exactly what we are experiencing.

When you are facing hardship, use Psalm 119 as a guide for how to walk through it. First, give thanks: "It is good for me that I have been afflicted, that I may learn Your statutes." Second, read the Word. Third, pray for God to be your "hiding place" and your protection. Fourth, pray for deliverance: "Consider my affliction and deliver me, for I do not forget Your law."

PRAYING WHEN TRIALS ARE LONG

Hear my prayer, O Lord,
and let my cry come to You.
Do not hide Your face from me in the day of my trouble;
incline Your ear to me;
in the day that I call, answer me speedily.

PSALM 102:1–2

IN THE BEGINNING OF PSALM 102, THE AUTHOR is desperate. He has been suffering for a while, and he needs deliverance now. He asks the Lord to hurry up! For the rest of the psalm he pours his heart out to God, telling Him exactly how painful and hard his life has been. By the end of his prayer he has found peace. He has found God to be his rock, and he has found the strength to continue praising God even in the middle of hardship, while waiting earnestly for God to deliver him.

21

In this psalm we are given additional words to pray as we ask for deliverance, and we are led to see the peace that comes when we draw near to God in a trial.

When a hardship drags on for a long time, we can easily grow weary and impatient. We want God to fix it immediately. We want answers, resolution, clarity. We start to feel desperate for deliverance. This kind of desperation or impatience will drive us somewhere. We may start Googling for advice or asking friends. We will most likely start complaining and talking about our struggle more than we should. Or we try to suppress the pain by any distraction we can find that numbs how we feel: drinking, smoking, overeating, watching too much TV, shopping, changing whatever we can in life. Impatience in trial takes away our ability to be content.

I remember one particularly emotional day during my teenage years. I was crying and having trouble articulating why. To me it seemed like everything was wrong with my life, and I didn't know where to start. My father, who is a writer and doctor of theology, calmly handed me a book about the theology of emotions called *The Cry of the Soul* by Dan Allender and Tremper Longman. The authors explain how to differentiate between emotions that are righteous and emotions that are destructive. But what stood out to me the most was their explanation of how God uses emotions to draw us to Himself. Our righteous emotions should be viewed as signals that we need to look to God. Often we try to suppress emotions with distractions instead of using them to build our relationship with the Lord.

The emotion of desperation in the middle of a tough time is a red flag that we need to run to God. If impatience drives us somewhere, we should let it drive us to the Lord. When we are impatient to be done with our trial, we need to look at what the psalmist does: he prays. He tells God exactly what he is feeling. He searches for answers in God instead of in the world. When we are weary, this emotion is like an empty light on the dashboard. We need more fuel, and we need to find it in His Word.

We can find our fuel by reading Scripture, making sure we have made regular reading part of our life. Maybe you have a quiet time set aside already each day. Can you fit in another one? Can you begin and end your day with time in the Word? Finding this time is not easy for many people, especially for busy parents who are always caring for another person. When I became a mother I started listening to Bible audio while I washed dishes and folded laundry. I listen to it while I am doing puzzles or coloring with my little ones, simultaneously training them to be quiet. Where can you find a few minutes in the Word? Do you have a long commute when you could listen to the Bible? Can you squeeze in a chapter to read aloud at breakfast, lunch, or dinner? We are also fed by regular prayer, both alone and in groups. We are fed by attending church weekly. We are fed by seeking counsel when needed from friends or professionals.

Even without leaving our homes, we can fuel up our souls by listening to sermons online or reading the best of the thousands of Christian books that have been written over the centuries. Learning about God is one of the most powerful ways to draw near to Him. Weariness is not a sin, but our response to it can be. Weariness is a signal telling us we need God and we need to find all the means of encouragement He has given us and to fill up on them.

By the end of Psalm 102, the writer has found peace and comfort. He reminds himself that his life is fading, but that God will never fade. Why does this bring him so much comfort? God does not change. We get tired and weary, but He stays the same. He has been delivering His people for all of history. He has been protecting them and blessing them and guiding them.

When trials are dragging on and you feel impatient, run towards to the Lord by praying these words: "Hear my prayer, O LORD, and let my cry come to You. Do not hide Your face from me in the day of my trouble; incline Your ear to me; in the day that I call, answer me speedily." Feed yourself with His Word so that you can rest in peace as you wait for His answer.

PRAYING WHEN WE ARE IN TROUBLE

Have mercy on me, O LORD for I am weak;
O LORD, heal me, for my bones are troubled.
My soul also is greatly troubled;
But You, O LORD——how long?
Return, O LORD, deliver me!
Oh, save me for Your mercies' sake!
For in death there is no remembrance of You;
in the grave who will give You thanks?

PSALM 6:2–5

AFTER EXPRESSIONS OF PRAISE, PLEADING for deliverance is the most common theme in the Book of Psalms. In many verses the author is begging God to remember him and asking God how long he must wait for deliverance. Running to God is a natural reaction for David when he is in trouble. He does not seek God quietly. David's heart is in anguish, and he is shouting out to God for help, demanding deliverance. He knows God, and he knows that God is merciful. He knows that God does deliver His people. He even points out to God that if He doesn't deliver him, then he will not be able to praise Him. How can David tell others of God's mercy and kindness if God doesn't show up with mercy and kindness? How can he praise God if he doesn't have life? This psalm gives us a specific reason to bring our troubles before the Lord: His deliverance brings Him glory.

Whether in a great trial or a small annoyance, we must run to God in the first place when we are troubled. It was about two weeks after my first baby was born when we discovered that she was very colicky. She screamed for hours every day and nothing would console her. She screamed when we rode in the car. She was especially difficult in crowds. When we left the house, she would cry the whole time. As a new mother, this was hard and confusing and frustrating. I wasn't sure what I was doing wrong, so I started to read all the baby books. They promised that if I followed their system then things would be easier. I learned how to swaddle, I cut every possible food allergen out of our diet, I tried letting her cry it out, I tried feeding her more, and I tried feeding her less. I spent months troubleshooting and reading and trying to control this little grumpy person. Do you know what I completely failed to do? I didn't pray specifically for help from God. I guess I thought it was too small a problem for God to care about, or that my maternal intuition should already know the answers. This is where

I got it all wrong. I looked to the "experts" instead of looking to God. What troubles are you facing in your life that seem too insignificant to bring before God? Are you dealing with an annoying coworker? Are you pressed for time and can't seem to accomplish what you need to in a day? Are you trying to manage your health or weight? Are you having a hard time balancing social life and family responsibilities? Before you search Amazon for a time management book, bring these things to God.

When trouble comes, big or small, our first reaction should be to cry out to God. If I truly believed that God was almighty and all powerful, if He was the One who creates babies and all their weird quirks, then why wouldn't I ask for His guidance as I was struggling? Are there struggles in your life that you have thought were too trivial for God? Do you have an unfair teacher or a sporadic boss or a lazy spouse? Do you have weight to lose or a credit card to pay off? We are often much more ready to seek help from other people than from God. When troubles start in our marriage, we are quicker to seek advice in books or friends than in prayer. We want a quick answer that comes with a promise of success. When health problems come, we are quicker to Google than to pray. Getting marriage advice and searching for ways to boost our health can be good gifts, but we should first seek the Creator of all things when we are confused about life.

In his book *The Problem of Pain*, C.S. Lewis writes, "God whispers to us in our pleasures, speaks to us in our conscience, but shouts in our pain: it is His megaphone to rouse a deaf world."* When we are in pain, God uses it to create a strong connection between us and Him. Prayers whispered in desperation are often more filled with faith than any other prayers. He uses our pain to rouse us to remember Him and how He has always been merciful.

When I look back at times that have been particularly difficult, in my memory they often feel dark. But this is not necessarily how God sees those times. He sees difficulties as opportunities for us to increase our faith in Him, and the quicker we are to run to Him, the quicker we are to see all His acts of mercy in all our trials. By the end of the psalm, David is letting us know how God responded to his desperate plea: "Depart from me, all you workers of iniquity; for the LORD has heard the voice of my weeping. The LORD has heard my supplication; the LORD will receive my prayer" (vv. 8–9).

The result of running to God in trouble is that He delivers. James says that trials make us perfect and complete, lacking nothing. If we lack the wisdom to see this, we only need to ask (James 1:4–5). God isn't looking for stoic prayers; He is looking for us to just ask. Do you need healing? Ask Him. Tell Him how painful it has been. Remind Him how hard it is for you to praise Him when you are in pain. Do you want children? Ask Him. Tell Him all the hard moments that remind you of your barrenness.

---

* C.S. Lewis, *The Problem of Pain* (1940; New York: HarperOne, 1996), 91.

Tell Him how heavy your heart feels and how fast the time is going. Are you tired of working a boring job? Tell Him how weary you are. Tell Him that you feel like your life and talents are being wasted. Do you have many children and you want sleep? Ask Him. Tell Him how hard it is to live a virtuous life when you have to drink five cups of coffee to make it through one day. Do you need money? Ask Him. Tell Him about how the debt weighs on you. Tell Him how difficult it is to rejoice when you have a weight like that on you. God wants His people to be rejoicing and He delights to deliver. Sometimes His deliverance brings us out of our storm and sometimes His deliverance meets us with grace in the storm. There are some struggles that God requires His people to face for a lifetime, but He will uphold them all the way with a delivering hand in the midst of the struggle.

What struggles are you facing today? As you pray for deliverance use the words David gave us: "O LORD–how long? Return, O LORD, deliver me! Oh, save me for Your mercies' sake!" Remind God that your deliverance brings glory to Him: "Oh, save me for Your mercies' sake! For in death there is no remembrance of You; in the grave who will give You thanks?"

PRAYING WHEN WE ARE OVERWHELMED

Lord, all my desire is before You;
and my sighing is not hidden from You.
My heart pants, my strength fails me;
as for the light of my eyes, it also has gone from me.
PSALM 38:9–10

WAITING FOR THE LORD IS HARD. IT IS hard to continually pray for the same thing when it feels like no progress is being made. It is hard to continue to have faith and trust when our prayers are not being answered the way we want and God is asking us to keep waiting. We can get discouraged and hopeless. What does David do when he starts to feel this way? In Psalm 38, he is feeling God's anger because of his sin. He is lonely, and his friends have abandoned him. Not only is his situation causing him mental distress, but it is also causing him physical distress and pain. He has begged

the Lord for help, and the Lord has not answered. In the
final verse, he asks the Lord to hurry up! David does
not come to God in prayer attempting to hide how he
feels. He reminds God that He knows all of his desires:
He can see his sighing, his pain, his failing strength. He
tells God that even the light in his eyes has gone out. He
is losing motivation to live. In the previous chapters we
have seen different ways to approach the Lord and ask
for deliverance, but here we see the psalmist pouring out
his heart to God. His only reason for appeal is that he is
overwhelmed.

I find that I am often too proud to admit when I feel
this overwhelmed. Even though we are to rejoice and be
courageous in our afflictions, we need to remember that
God is our Father who cares about how we are doing.
He cares about our hearts, about our feelings, about our
desires. He cares when we are struggling, and He wants
to hear about it. We can give thanks for a trial, but in
the same prayer we should also remind Him to hurry
up and deliver us because our strength is growing thin.
It is humility to pour ourselves out to Him in this way,
to admit that we cannot get through hard times without
His help. It is also a comfort to pray this way and to tell
Him our pain and to know that He hears. It comforts us
to have a person to go to when we are spent. This is how
we allow Him to shoulder the burden of our pain. If we
believe that God is our Savior and Protector who loves
us, we will not be hesitant to pour ourselves out hon-
estly to Him. Our faith in His goodness drives us to tell

Him that we are at the end of our rope, that we can't see a light at the end of the tunnel, that we need Him to help us immediately, that we are frustrated and confused.

Have you ever felt like God was taking away everything you wanted in your life? Have you felt like things were empty and pointless, or every day just felt hard? All the things that used to bring you joy are gone, or all the goals you had hoped to accomplish have disintegrated. This is not an uncommon theme in Christian stories. God often allows pain in our life so that our focus will not be on things of this world. He often allows us to stay in a trial for a long time to the point where nothing brings us joy except turning to Him. This is a great mercy. God does not get offended that we wanted all those other things first. He does not reject us because we looked for satisfaction or joy other places before we ran to Him. He welcomes us even though we come to Him as our last resort, and even though when we finally come to Him we are exhausted and overwhelmed and weary. C.S. Lewis describes this kindness well:

> If God were proud He would hardly have us on such terms [as a last resort], but He is not proud. He stoops to conquer, He will have us even though we have shown that we prefer everything else to Him, and come to Him because there is 'nothing better' to be had.*

* C.S. Lewis, *Problem of Pain*, 96.

Many people get married young, thinking that romantic love will make them happy. They find quickly that it is harder than they thought it would be. Many people seek their dream career, not allowing anything to stand in their way, and they find it is not as satisfying as they imagined it would be. I know many women who thought that becoming a mother would satisfy their neediness, only to find that it drains them even more. The problem is that seeking after God and glorifying Him with every decision was not the main focus all along. But even so, God welcomes us.

He is patient, and He waits for us to get to the end of our rope, when we realize that we actually can't get through this life without Him. He is not so proud that He will push us away or condemn us for trying to live by our own strength. He welcomes us and offers a kind ear. He welcomes us and offers us the real food that will really make us strong. He offers us Himself, bread and wine, broken to give us strength.

Are you overwhelmed and weary? Lay your frustration out to God and pray the words of David: "Lord, all my desire is before You; and my sighing is not hidden from You. My heart pants, my strength fails me; as for the light of my eyes, it also has gone from me."

PRAYING WHEN GOD
IS SILENT

My God, My God, why have You forsaken Me?
Why are You so far from helping Me,
and from the words of My groaning?
O My God, I cry in the daytime, but You do not hear;
and in the night season, and am not silent.
But You are holy, enthroned in the praises of Israel.
Our fathers trusted in You;
they trusted, and You delivered them.
They cried to You, and were delivered;
they trusted in You, and were not ashamed.

PSALM 22:1–5

THE WORDS THAT CHRIST CRIED OUT ON the cross are from Psalm 22: "My God, my God, why have You forsaken Me?" In His worst moment of agony, He felt alone and separated from His Father. David knew what this was like. Chased all over the country by his bitter father-in-law Saul, betrayed by his son Absalom, overwhelmed with the grief of losing his best friend and his sons, David was a man who was no stranger to suffering. In this psalm we see a desperate plea for deliverance, and we see the acknowledgement that if suffering is here, it feels as though God is not. Here we see the psalmist appealing for deliverance by reminding God of His past deliverances.

When we are in the middle of a particularly tough time, it often feels like we have been abandoned by God. When a loved one is in a car accident, we find ourselves crying out, "Lord, where were you?" When we watch parents slip away because of cancer or other diseases, we beg Him to heal them, and it feels like He is silent. When we are in major financial devastation, when we have a child who rejects the faith, when we are diagnosed with a chronic illness, we ask Him, "Why are You so far from helping me?" It feels like our prayers for miracles and blessings are falling on deaf ears.

Jesus says that turning to God in our dark times is an act of faith, and continuing to come to Him, unabashed by His silence, shows that we believe. In Matthew 15, a Canaanite woman comes to Jesus and begs Him to heal her demon-possessed daughter. Jesus responds by saying, "I was not sent except to the lost sheep of the house of Israel" (v. 24). He is telling her that He was there to perform miracles for and to save the Jews, not the Canaanites. He then calls her a dog, saying that the bread is for the children, meaning the Jews. But she doesn't leave. She does not let it go. She says, "Yes, Lord, yet even the little dogs eat the crumbs which fall from their masters' table" (v. 27). She knows she isn't one of God's chosen people, but she knows that God is good and that He shows mercy even to the undeserving. Do you remember what Jesus calls her begging and arguing? He calls it faith. Actually, He calls it *great* faith, and He heals her daughter immediately.

David begs like this Canaanite woman. He reminds God of the past when the forefathers trusted in Him, and He delivered them. He remembers the stories, and he remembers God's help. He knows about Moses at the Red Sea and Abraham on Mount Moriah, and he reminds God of His mercy then. In the same way, the Canaanite woman is saying, "I know You are good. I know You are merciful. I know that You cannot be anything other than kind to those who call on You. So, help me, because that is what You do." When we are in great trouble, it is by faith that we turn to God, especially when it feels like He has forgotten about us. It is by faith that we ask Him continually for help. It is by faith that we point out to Him that He seems to be ignoring us. It is by faith that we remind Him that it isn't in His character to leave His people in trouble. It is by faith that we remind Him to come and help because He always does.

When my husband and I were moving from Idaho to Kentucky, due to a variety of circumstances we were without a job, without savings, and, thanks to a last-minute miscommunication while on the road, without an apartment lined up at our destination. We were literally broke and homeless, and my husband was suffering from a strange illness. To top it all off, the transmission in our car started going out somewhere in Montana, and we had two tiny daughters in the back seat. It was so risky and terrifying that it felt surreal, but God showed up at the last minute and we didn't spend any nights on the streets of Louisville. He provided a job that paid more than we had anticipated, He provided an apartment, He healed my husband, and He provided a community of His people to greet us with cookies and help us move when we arrived. When God is silent and I see waves start to swell around us again, I often remind Him of that deliverance. The goodness that He showed before is the goodness that He will show again. Tell Him when you feel like your prayers are hitting the ceiling, and find encouragement in remembering that He is the One who has always made sure that even the dogs have crumbs.

Look back over your own story. When has God shown up and helped when you were on the edge of disaster? Remind Him of those times and ask Him to do it again by praying Psalm 22: "O My God, I cry in the daytime, but You do not hear; and in the night season, and am not silent. But You are holy, enthroned in the praises of Israel. Our fathers trusted in You; they trusted, and You delivered them."

REMINDING GOD OF
HIS PROMISES

Lord, where are Your former lovingkindnesses,
which You swore to David in Your truth?
PSALM 89:49

PSALM 89 WAS WRITTEN BY ETHAN THE
Ezrahite. Within the psalm he offers praise to God for
continually showing mercy to His people, especially to
David. He reminds God how He has always remem-
bered His covenant with His people. He lists many of
God's promises, and in verse 49 we see him asking God
why He doesn't seem to be fulfilling His promises now.

There are times in our lives when it may feel like God
is not fulfilling His promises. In Isaiah 41:13 it says, "For
I, the LORD your God, will hold your right hand, saying to
you, 'Fear not, I will help you.'" Even though God promises to be with us when we are in trouble, sometimes

we still feel alone. Proverbs 10:4 says, "He who has a slack hand becomes poor, but the hand of the diligent makes rich." Even though this verse says that the diligent will be made rich, sometimes godly men work hard and are still poor. Philippians 4:7 says, "And the peace of God, which surpasses all understanding, will guard your hearts and minds through Christ Jesus." The peace of God is supposed to be with us if we cast our cares on Him, but sometimes worry and anxiety linger.

When it appears to us like God has forgotten His promises, we should continue to remind Him. We should continue to pray, reminding Him that He loves us, that He promises to hear us, that He cares for us, that He promises peace, that He promises to answer our prayers, that He promises to forgive us. When we are praying for deliverance and deliverance does not seem to come, we need to remind God that He has promised to deliver us. "I will deliver you from the hand of the wicked, and I will redeem you from the grip of the terrible" (Jeremiah 15:21).

The Psalms are full of pleas for God to remember what He has already promised to do. We glorify Him when we remind Him of His Word. It shows Him that we believe what He said, and that our faith in His Word is strong. He gives us many things to help us keep His promises at the forefront of our minds, but most importantly He gives us the Eucharist. The bread and wine remind us of Christ's death and resurrection, and whenever we partake of them we are reminded that God comes to save, that He remembers His promise, and that He does not go back on His Word. When we eat, we are becoming part of Christ, and we are given the power to stand on Christ's righteousness and ask God to remember His promises to us for the sake of His Son's holiness.

Reminding God of His promises is as much an encouragement for us as it is an act of faith. If we have a sick child, we remind God of His love for our child and remind Him that He promises deliverance. We are encouraged and God is glorified by our faith. When Jesus heals, He often tells the sick that their faith is great. He is not surprised that they are needy. He is pleased that they come to Him for help and that they believe He is there to fulfill the words of the prophets. Remind yourself of God's promises daily, and when you pray in a trial, you will easily remember all the promises He has given to you. He has said, "I will never leave you nor forsake you" (Heb. 13:5). Memorize words like these and believe them. He wants them written on your heart to give you hope.

When God seems slow to fulfill His promises, boldly cry out to Him with these words: "Lord, where are Your former lovingkindnesses, which You swore to David in Your truth?" This is faith.

REMEMBERING GOD'S GOODNESS IN PRAYER

I remember the days of old;
I meditate on all Your works;
I muse on the work of Your hands.
I spread out my hands to You;
My soul longs for You like a thirsty land...
Revive me, O LORD, for Your name's sake!
For Your righteousness' sake bring my soul out of trouble.

PSALM 143:5–6, 11

IN PSALM 143, DAVID IS AGAIN PRAYING for deliverance from God, and he specifically prays for guidance towards righteousness. He asks that he would be rescued from his current trial, but also that God would show him the next step. He doesn't just ask for a quick solution; he also asks for what to do when he is delivered. In verse 8, he says, "Cause me to know the way in which I should walk, for I lift up my soul to

You." He is confident that God will hear him and listen to him. In verse 11, he asks that God would save him "for Your righteousness' sake." He is asking God to protect His own reputation by rescuing the ones who place their faith in Him. When God rescues His servants, it speaks loudly to others about God's righteousness. When Daniel was saved from the lions, King Darius declared that Daniel's God was the true God. God's deliverance of those who love Him proves His love, but it also demonstrates His character.

God cannot be anything other than what He is. He can never be not good. This is what David reminds Him when he prays. He is asking God to be true to His character, which is always good. When we imitate David's prayer, we are showing that we have faith in His goodness. When we remind God that He is the Healer, the Deliverer, the Comforter, we are showing Him that we believe He can heal us, deliver us, and comfort us.

Reminding God of His character also reminds *us* of His character. If we pray, "Remember that You healed me from my last sickness; please heal me again," this gives us hope because we remember that He is good and that He is a healer. Reminding God of His righteousness strengthens our faith and hope in Him. Remembering God's character is a great act of faith, and we see this throughout all the Psalms. The historical psalms recall all the times that God has rescued His people. The personal psalms of David are full of remembering God's kindness in the past, which fuels hope for the future.

Deuteronomy 6:6–7 says, "And these words which I command you today shall be in your heart. You shall teach them diligently to your children, and shall talk of them when you sit in your house, when you walk by the way, when you lie down, and when you rise up."

The Israelites were commanded to remember. They were commanded to do whatever it took to keep God's Words in their hearts and minds. Remembering is one of the most important ways for a follower of Christ to keep his faith strong. At our church we partake in the Eucharist weekly, commemorating Christ's death and resurrection, actively and regularly remembering together. When we hand the bread and wine to our children, we tell them to remember. This protects us from fear because we recall God's goodness in the past, and this gives hope to our faith. When we remember God's faithfulness in the Eucharist, we are also calling upon Him to remember. The bread and wine are as much a reminder for Him as they are for us. He has set up the sacrament as a reminder for Himself that we are His people whom He has promised to save.

When we remind God, we remind ourselves. David's prayer for God's remembrance is preceded by a detailed list of what kind of goodness David is hoping to receive from God. He wants to hear God's love first thing in the morning, he wants direction and guidance for his life, he wants deliverance from his enemies, he wants protection, he wants teaching, and he wants to be led in righteousness (verses 8–10). He is confident that because he can remember God always being righteous, He will be righteous again, and He will grant David all of His requests.

Remember how God has shown kindness to you in the past. As you bring your requests to Him, remind Him of all the good things He has done and, like David, ask Him to remember these things to preserve His own reputation by praying, "Revive me, O Lord, for Your name's sake! For Your righteousness' sake bring my soul out of trouble."

PRAYING FOR CONTENTMENT

Nevertheless I am continually with You;
You hold me by my right hand.
You will guide me with Your counsel,
and afterward receive me to glory.
Whom have I in heaven but You?
And there is none upon earth that I desire besides You.

PSALM 73:23–26

PSALM 73 IS WRITTEN BY ASAPH, WHO WAS a teacher and music leader in the court of David. He is confused and grieved by the prosperity of the wicked. He sees men all around him who appear to have blessings, and yet he has suffering. He struggles to find peace and contentment with his own circumstances, especially when those who do not love God are prospering. Within the psalm, he finds the answer to his frustration. He sees that the end of the wicked is destruction, and all their wealth and success is merely wind. He sees that fellowship with God is far sweeter than anything in this earth. He finds rest and contentment in trusting the story God is writing because he remembers that the end is glory.

J.C. Ryle said, "Few, I am afraid, have the least idea what a shortcut to happiness it is to be content."* If we struggle with happiness, an easy answer is to find contentment with our current circumstances. When we are content, we can more clearly see how God is working within all sorts of situations.

Jeremiah Burroughs, in his book *The Rare Jewel of Christian Contentment,* defines contentment as "that sweet, inward, quiet, gracious frame of spirit, which freely submits to and delights in God's wise and fatherly disposal in every condition."† Richard Swenson in his book *Contentment* says, "Contentment is believing that God's provision is enough for our physical needs, that His presence is enough for our emotional needs, and that His providence is enough for our future needs."‡ Contentment is believing that a good and kind Father is intricately working out the details of our lives, which results in a deep peace and quietness and strength in our souls.

* "Be Content," in 109 *Sermons and Other Works* (Monergism Books, 2011).
† Jeremiah Burroughs, *The Rare Jewel of Christian Contentment* (London: W. Bentley, 1651), 3.
‡ *Contentment: The Secret to a Lasting Calm* (Colorado Springs: NavPress, 2013), Kindle loc. 132.

This is the kind of peace that we see Asaph coming to in Psalm 73. He comes to rest in his heart because he trusts that the Lord is using the lives of the wicked to tell a good story. Asaph surrenders himself to God. He declares that there is nothing in the world he desires more than God. His union with God trumps all his other desires. This is the path of contentment. It is not some kind of pious self-denial, but rather it means loving God more than all the other things that you love. Contentment doesn't mean that you have no loves and no desires. Yahweh is not Buddha, and He does not want you to empty yourself of desire. He wants you to love Him more than those desires. We see David telling God about his own desires many times in the Psalms, but his complaints are not a lack of contentment. His complaints to God are a testimony of his faith because he is offering his desire to God. When we looked at Psalm 38 we saw David saying, "Lord, all my desire is before You; and my sighing is not hidden from You" (v. 9). It was not a sin for David to desire or to sigh. He offered his hope and his disappointment to God. He knew that God was the only One who could fulfill his desire and answer his complaint.

A few weeks after I moved to Kentucky with my husband, I was offered a job at Southern Seminary. I loved it. It was fast-paced with lots of variety and delightful people to work with. But after working only six months, I could see the stress it was placing on my children and my husband. My husband's workload was increasing by that time, and it was becoming clear that I needed to give up my work. It was a hard transition to give up a job that I loved and move back into full-time motherhood. On one of my last days of work I went to one of the small prayer chapels on the campus of the seminary for a few quiet minutes before heading home. The sun was illuminating the stained glass window and reflecting colorful lights around the room. Someone had left a Bible on the bench, open to Psalm 73. The Spirit brought those words to me that day to remind me that God would be with me continually, that He was holding me by my right hand, that He was guiding me, that He was leading me on a path that leads to glory. Could I let go of all these desires to pursue my work? Could I say that He was the only thing I desired? Could I find my identity in following His lead instead of in my job? Could I be content with Him? Could I be content to let Him tell my story even if it didn't seem to be going the way I wanted? I ran full-force in the direction that He was leading, and I found that my contentment grew as I sought Him.

To experience the peace and joy that is real contentment, we have to pray for a biblical understanding of trials and embrace Paul's perspective on afflictions and sufferings. We have to become un-American and stop seeing trials as an interruption in our fulfillment of a good life. We have to stop questioning God's love for us just because we have a bumpy road to walk. When we see ourselves as characters in a beautiful story that God is writing, we can see more clearly what He is doing.

Everything evil that we face is ultimately anti-God: death, sickness, slander, pain, etc. He hates all those things. They are part of a bigger story in which they are being defeated. The hardships are ultimately taken from us and nailed to the cross through Jesus. All our losses are ultimately restored. The trials are valleys that lead to higher mountains, evils that prepare us for greater goodness, pain that makes us ready for the weight of glory we are promised. When we are truly able to see these things as part of God's story, as the good parts of a story that He is working for us and through us, we are able to have open hearts to be content. Then we will be able to say with Asaph that we really have no other desires on this earth, that God is our guide, holding us by the right hand.

Are you struggling to be content? Are you struggling to accept the story that God is writing for you? Remember that God is leading you carefully, gently, lovingly on the road to glory. Willingly lay down your desires to follow His lead and tell Him in prayer, "Besides You, I desire nothing on this earth."

ASKING FOR BLESSING

God be merciful to us and bless us,
and cause His face to shine upon us, *Selah*,
that Your way may be known on earth,
Your salvation among all nations.

PSALM 67:1–2

JESUS SAYS THAT WE SHOULD NOT STORE up treasures on earth where moth and rust destroy, but that we should store our treasures in heaven (Matthew 6:20). This often gets misinterpreted to mean that God wants His people to be poor. This thinking creates false guilt over the desire that God would bless us with financial stability, with homes, with transportation, with clothing. It creates virtue out of poverty. Jesus did not come to make sure all His people lived poverty-stricken lives. He tells us to be generous because He wants our hearts to be directed towards others and towards God, not towards our wealth. Paul says that the love of money is the root of all kinds of evil; money itself is not evil (1 Timothy 6:10). When our hearts are set on increasing our wealth, when we are obsessed with it, counting it constantly, hoarding it, grasping for it, sacrificing friendships for it, then it has become our god. But this does not mean that we are always supposed to be poor. We should pray for God to bless us so that we can do work for His glory in this world.

Psalm 67 praises God because of His generous blessing towards His people. Blessings come in so many forms. Some are blessed with many children, some with financial wealth, some with beautiful houses and land, some with amazing skill sets. Whatever the means, God always blesses His people, and we learn from Psalm 67 that blessing is something we should pray for and hope for. This includes financial blessing. I believe that it is godly and wise to pray that the Lord would increase us both in numbers and in wealth. In any kind of ministry there are always leaders praying for funds, for facilities, for numbers. This should be the same in the ministry of family. We should pray for financial stability, for homes, for children and grandchildren and great-grandchildren. Pray that the Lord makes us great.

Verse 2 tells us why: "That Your way may be known on the earth, your salvation among the nations." We can hope and pray for blessing because when the faithful increase, God's Word is made known all over the earth. When we raise godly children, they are arrows that go out into the world to spread the good news. When we use our money to show hospitality and to care for one another, it spreads the good news to the world that God is love. When we are blessed, and we use it rightly, it makes His name great on the earth.

This only works if we are being good stewards of our blessings. If we are blessed financially, but we give none of it to the poor, how is that increasing glory to God's name? If we have twelve children but we don't spend time loving them and educating them, they will not grow up to be a blessing to His kingdom. If we are stingy with our giving to the Church, how can the Church increase? The Church is God's army on earth to spread the gospel and conquer the world. Our gifts to the Church show that our hearts are passionate for the expansion of the gospel.

This should be our motivation to pray for blessing. We should strive to be stable financially, to care for our families, to give them good homes, to give them good clothing, to give to the Church generously, so that the world will know what kind of God we serve. We serve a God who cares for children, who feeds, who clothes, who covers medical bills. We should want blessing so that we can be great on the earth, because when we are full of God's love in our actions, our greatness points to His greatness, and this in turn saves the world.

The psalmist is bold to ask for blessing. When you have a need, pray using the words of Psalm 67: "God be merciful to us and bless us, and cause His face to shine upon us, Selah, that Your way may be known on earth, Your salvation among all nations."

REMEMBERING GOD'S GENEROSITY IN PRAYER

For a day in Your courts is better than a thousand.
I would rather be a doorkeeper in the house of my God
than dwell in the tents of wickedness.
For the LORD God is a sun and shield;
the LORD will give grace and glory;
no good thing will He withhold
from those who walk uprightly.

PSALM 84:10–11

PSALM 84 IS WRITTEN BY THE SONS OF
Korah, recounting many wonderful things that the Lord
has done. They tell about His goodness in creation and
how He shows His love to those who go through life
trusting in Him. In verses 10 and 11, they say that there
is no better place than to be in the courts of the Lord

because He does not withhold any good thing from the righteous, and they have seen this.

God is generous to His people. He loves to shower us with things that we do not deserve and then offer even more gifts than we could possibly imagine. He gives us sun and sand, lattes and whipped cream, beautiful snow and sunsets, flowers and rain, bacon and chocolate. He gives us families and friends and churches and schools and community. He also gives joy and peace and purpose and courage and faith and hope and grace and glory. The sons of Korah know God to be generous in all these ways, and that is one of the things that drives them to find one day in His courts more appealing than a thousand anywhere else. God is overflowing with goodness, and those who see His generosity do not stop chasing after Him.

It is important that we imitate God's generosity, and most often this means being generous towards those that are closest to us, like our children. We need to provide all the basics for them: nutritious food, clean, well-fitting clothing, comfortable beds, medical attention when needed, consistent training. If we are to imitate God, we have to give even more than the basics. God is extremely generous, even to people who deserve none of it. It is kind to feed our children, but it is even kinder to let them help us cook and make their favorite meals. It is kind to provide dinner, but it is even kinder to light candles and set out a pretty tablecloth to show your family that you are excited to have them there.

It is kind to clothe your children, but it is even kinder to take them shopping and let them pick out what they like and guide them as they enter into the years of shopping on their own. To imitate God, we have to go above and beyond as He does. He is not worried about spoiling us. He knows when to gently teach us the lessons that we need to learn. He is extravagantly kind to His children. When you see that in your own life, you will overflow with generosity towards your children.

Christian children should grow up in homes that are saturated with generosity. We should always give a little extra time to them when they want to snuggle, a little extra care for them when they are sick. Maybe they want just one more back rub. We should seek to give their favorite nutritious snacks instead of the ones that are the most convenient for us. We should give our time to help them clean up messes so that they can have the opportunity to be creative. We should give our energy to bathe them regularly so that they can feel clean and cared for. If your children are grown, they need your generosity just as much as they always have. If you are not a parent, who is close to you that you can be generous towards? Can you help your parents? Can you bless a coworker or a neighbor? Can you go beyond what is expected of you? If God is like this, then this is how we should be. God is generous even with grace. When we give a little more of ourselves, He gives us more grace. When we imitate His generosity, we start seeing more and more how generous He has been to us. Our gratitude grows, and God is greatly glorified.

Have you been tempted to think that God has been stingy with you? Have you been tempted to be stingy with others in serving them? When you pray, remind God that He is the God who withholds "no good thing" from His people. Ask Him to give you the same attitude of generosity towards those around you.

PRAYING FOR OUR WORK

And let the beauty of the LORD our God be upon us,
and establish the work of our hands for us;
yes, establish the work of our hands.

PSALM 90:17

MOSES WROTE PSALM 90 AS A BEAUTIFUL prayer about the expanse of life. He talks about how short our life is and how futile it feels. He asks God for blessing, and he acknowledges that God's wrath over our sin will consume us unless we are shown mercy. In the final verses, he prays for God's beauty to rest upon us, and that God would establish the works of our hands. We need God's beauty to be on us because we are sinful. We need God to establish our works, because without His blessing our works are nothing more than fleeting moments that mean nothing. We need God to take our feeble work and make something great and meaningful out of it. We can't create meaningful work on our own.

61

There is something I have noticed to be a common struggle for Christians as they enter into middle adulthood. When we are first beginning adulthood, our goals seem very attainable and optimistic: we want to raise godly families, give generously to our church, be involved in our communities, work jobs that make a difference in the world. We have plans and goals and dreams, and many of them seem possible as we start in on the work. But after a few children and lots of sleep deprivation, years of working the job we only planned to have for a few months, feeling like we are just living to survive, many Christians get discouraged. It seems like those original dreams are not getting any closer and that our work to expand the kingdom is feeble. But take heart! Psalm 90 tells us that God will establish the work of our hands.

The race that Paul refers to in 1 Corinthians 9 is not an easy one, it is challenging. If you have children, it feels like you are running this race on wet cement. We need to look to God to give us motivation, direction, and purpose with our mundane, fast-paced, normal lives. We need to know that He is taking our works, however small they may seem, and establishing them, making them into something great. We need to believe that He is taking all those middle-of-the-night newborn feedings and creating something good from them. We need to believe that He is taking all those hundreds of hours of computer programing and making them great.

Octavius Winslow, a nineteenth-century evangeli-
cal preacher, said, "Wherever you are, God has work for
you to do, a purpose through you to be accomplished, in
which He blends your happiness with His glory."* If we
are at home with children, or teaching in a tiny startup
school, or scrubbing toilets, or chopping wood, or in meet-
ings all day, or driving a garbage truck, God has a purpose
for us there. He has a plan to work the current events to
bring us happiness and to bring Him glory. Don't despise
work, even if it is something you don't care to be doing.
Whatever work is right in front of you is the work that
God has given which He plans to establish for greatness.
All the stories you read to your children, all the driveways
you shovel in the winter, all the work emails you send, are
small seeds that God will use to create great things if we
do them in faith. The key

In his exhortation to the slaves in Colossians 3:23–
24, Paul writes, "And whatever you do, do it heartily, as
to the Lord and not to men, knowing that from the Lord
you will receive the reward of the inheritance; for you
serve the Lord Christ."

God loves to take small works of service done in faith,
offered to Him, and reward them greatly. Even if we have
hit a point in our life where we see that we have not accomplished the goals we had hoped to, our faith is in
the reward.

---

* Octavius Winslow, *Divine realities; or, spiritual reflections for the
saint and sinner* (London: John F. Shaw, 1860), 61.

Are you tired? Do you find that your daily activities seem mundane? Find hope in praying these words of Moses: "Establish the work of our hands for us; yes, establish the work of our hands."

PRAYING FOR
OUR WORDS

Set a guard, O LORD, over my mouth;
keep watch over the door of my lips.
PSALM 141:3

IN PSALM 141, DAVID IS PRAYING FOR
protection from wickedness. He asks specifically in verse
3 for protection over his mouth, that whatever comes
out of his lips would be wise. This is a practice I have
been adopting more frequently. Before guests come for
dinner, before I have coffee with a friend, before I make
a phone call, before I sit down for dinner with my family, I pray that God would set a guard over my mouth.
I ask that my words would be kind, encouraging, but
also true. In our culture of increasing social media, it is
important to understand that our cyber and text words
are just as important as the words that come out of our

mouths. I read far too many status updates on Facebook that are dripping with complaining and discontent, often things that people would never say in person. We need to take a lesson from David and pray about our words, both spoken and typed.

God cares very much about our words. John 1:1 tells us that at the very beginning the Word was with God, and the Word was God. Our ability to use words is what sets us apart from other creatures, showing that we reflect the image of God. God used words to create the world. Words bring things into being: we create conflict or peace with our words, we create courage or fear with our words, we create action or discouragement with our words. Words also give life to our feelings. Jesus tells us in Matthew 12:34 that our words are the visible sign of what is in our hearts: "How can you, being evil, speak good things? For out of the abundance of the heart the mouth speaks." What we say with our mouths or type with our hands, reveals what thoughts we are entertaining in our minds and what emotions we are harboring in our hearts. When we speak, our emotions and opinions and thoughts take form and go out to either harm or encourage.

David continues in Psalm 141 to pray for discipline in other areas of his life. He describes "rebuke" and "striking" as kindnesses that set him on the path of righteousness (verse 5). He knows that righteousness in one area of life breeds righteousness in another area. When we are faithful and disciplined with one thing, the same kind of faithfulness will automatically start overflowing into other areas of our lives. In the same way, when we are undisciplined and unfaithful in small areas of our life, we will be lazy and foolish in many other areas. If we are undisciplined with our time, it often follows that we are undisciplined with our money. If we are undisciplined in caring for our homes and bodies, it often follows that we are lazy in disciplining and caring for our children. If we are undisciplined with our thoughts, it will absolutely follow that we will be undisciplined with our words.

Jesus gives us a helpful footing to learn how to have a guard over our words. We must first set a guard over our hearts. Proverbs 4:23 says, "Keep your heart with all vigilance, for from it flow the springs of life" (ESV). Our hearts are the source of our desires and feelings, and our care for them results in what we create with our words. Discipline starts with what we feed our hearts. We must fill our hearts with seeds that will produce good fruit: reading and memorizing Scripture regularly, reading encouraging books and blogs, listening to good sermons or conferences or podcasts, fellowshipping with wise friends. These seeds will grow to bear the fruit of encouraging, wise words.

We also have to be watchful and careful for weeds that choke out the fruit. We have to be on alert and pay attention to what thoughts are passing through our minds, and especially to what thoughts we allow to linger in our minds. We can have a passing thought of worry, a sinking feeling in our gut. We have a choice to continue to dwell on it, playing out each awful possibility in our minds, or we can choose to trust the Lord and actively think about something else. This takes practice. It is helpful to take note of what times and places we tend to let our thoughts become undisciplined, because this is when we let our hearts and emotions become affected by thoughts that are not nurturing.

At the end of the day, when I am tired from caring for children, it is particularly hard for me to control thoughts of fear, worry, and regret. When I am working with my hands without any conversation, like washing dishes or cleaning or folding laundry, it is easy to let my thoughts wander to discontent or worry. My thoughts will feed lies to my heart, and my heart will overflow with lying words if I am not careful. I have to set up active things to think about during these times. I can set a memory verse above the kitchen sink, or pray for my children while folding their tiny clothes, or listen to a sermon while cleaning the bathrooms. Our thoughts change our emotions, and our emotions change our words, and our words create action in the world. We have to actively be at war against sin in our thoughts. When our thoughts are full of sweetness, then the overflow from our mouths will be sweet. When we have disciplined our minds, then our words will be wise.

Consider times that you allow thoughts of fear or bitterness or discontent or doubt to rest in your mind. Remember that our thoughts birth our words, and our words bring life or death to the world around us. Pray for discipline in your mind and protection over your words by using Psalm 141: "Set a guard, O Lord, over my mouth; keep watch over the door of my lips."

PART II

PRAISING
with the PSALMS

INTRODUCTION

THE PSALMS TEACH US ABOUT THE CHARACTER
of God. Learning about God is integral to knowing how
to praise Him. We can easily praise God and offer Him
thanks for the things we see in our lives: our family, our
home, our job, our health. But when we know about
the character of God, we can thank Him for who He is.
In the Psalms we learn that He is merciful and that He
brings salvation and deliverance from sorrow. We learn
that He deals bountifully and showers blessings on his
people. We learn that it is not a burden for God to hear
from us when we beg Him for help. He does consider
us. We learn how to praise Him for these things, and
praise is the calling of the righteous (Ps. 33:1).

Praising God is an expression of gratitude. We are
declaring the glory that He is, but we are also thanking Him for being what He is. When we express gratitude, we change our reality. Focusing on bitterness and

resentment creates a reality of despair, but focusing on offering thanks and praise creates a reality of joy. As Proverbs 15:15 says, "All the days of the afflicted are evil, but he who is of a merry heart has a continual feast." Gratitude opens our eyes to see the glory of God surrounding us.

One of the major themes in the Psalms is remembrance. When the psalmist prays, he is often asking God to remember that He is good. When the psalmist praises, he is remembering all the good God has done for him. As you read through these psalms of praise, you will notice that the writers often recount historical events. Psalm 136 recounts the story of the Exodus from Egypt, but almost every other line is "for His mercy endures forever." The writer of the psalm is praising God for each act of mercy that He showed in the Exodus. As you work through these psalms of praise, think about how you can recount each turn in your story and praise God for it as the psalmist does.

The Psalms of praise are also very repetitive. Psalm 136 and Psalm 118 are good examples of this. Almost every verse in these psalms concludes with a praise such as "His mercy endures forever." In this section we learn how to praise like the psalmist. He does not stop with one expression of gratitude, but continues all day to thank God for what He has given and to praise Him for who He is. Dietrich Bonhoeffer wrote, "The words which come from God become, then, the steps on which we find our way to God."* God gives us the words to praise Him, and when we use those words, we are brought closer to Him. Our obedient response to Him always blesses us. Be repetitive in your praise. God does not grow tired of hearing it, and He uses praise and gratitude to nourish your soul.

* Dietrich Bonhoeffer, *Psalms: The Prayer Book of the Bible*, 12.

GOD'S GIFT OF JOY

When the LORD brought back the captivity of Zion,
we were like those who dream.
Then our mouth was filled with laughter,
and our tongue with singing.
Then they said among the nations,
"The LORD has done great things for them."
The LORD has done great things for us, and we are glad.

PSALM 126:1–3

PSALM 126 IS A PRAISE TO GOD FOR THE deliverance from captivity. It is written as a reminder to the Israelites of God's faithfulness to them, even though their captivity was a result of their unfaithfulness. When the Lord delivers, there is great rejoicing and all the nations can see how excellent God is.

There are two types of deliverance: eternal and present. Eternal deliverance is the salvation from sins, the resurrection of our bodies, and the coming of Christ's kingdom on earth. Eternal deliverance is the foundation of faith for every Christian. There is another kind of deliverance that is more immediate. I will call it present deliverance. It is the kind of salvation from things we experience in this life: deliverance from sickness, freedom from besetting sin, healing from emotional wounds. It extends to any answer to prayer. God offers both kinds of deliverance. He offers eternal life for those who believe in Him, and this we take on faith because we cannot see it with our eyes. He also offers present help in the short-term struggles that we have in this life. This doesn't mean that everything we pray for is always resolved right away, but we know that He is powerful and able to heal. He is willing to heal any kind of pain if it will be for our good, and He offers many passages of hope in His Word. When Israel was in captivity, it was a real, tangible, present pain that they were experiencing, being unable to have freedom and a home. God delivered them, which gave them the great joy that is recounted in Psalm 126. God loves to give joy, and He does this by offering real, tangible, present deliverance.

Sometimes we do not feel joyful. Newly converted Christians always comment on how joyful they feel after they give their life to Christ, but years of faithful service to Christ can be spotted with periods of joylessness. When we do not feel joyful, it is usually because we are allowing weeds to grow in our hearts, weeds of worry, regret, fear, envy, anger, or some other sin. Even in the middle of trials we can have joy if we do not give a foothold to worry and fear. These things rob us of joy when we allow our minds to be taken over by the worst-case scenario, instead of letting our minds be ruled by hope.

God wants His people to be joyful. He wants glad, rejoicing saints. This is why 1 Peter 5:7 says to cast all your cares on God. He cares for you, and cares about what happens to you. He can see the future, He is writing your story, and He is the great Deliverer. He wants us to let Him take care of both the immediate future and the eternal future. He is present and omnipresent. He is telling us not to worry or be afraid, but to be glad and rejoice. I know as well as anyone how hard the command to rejoice always can be. Negativity is like an old, comfortable shoe. It is easy to throw it on without even thinking. We have to engage in an active fight against worry, fear, and any other negative thoughts about the future. God says we are to cast those thoughts onto Him. We are not permitted to allow fears to run around in our minds. Whatever cares we have, He wants them given over in prayer. He doesn't want our minds brooding over them all day and night. He knows how easily these things steal our joy, and walking in obedience means that we do not allow them to take hold of us. We have to hold up a shield of faith to protect ourselves from the fiery darts of worry, fear, anxiety, and the lie that God will not deliver us.

God is the One who loves to deliver us from real and present problems because He loves to see His children shouting with joy. Our joy is a witness to the world that we follow the Deliverer, that we are in covenant with the

One who can solve any problem. Our joy comes because we know we are safe with Him. This confuses an anxiety-driven world. It is the way to show the world that "the Lord has done great things for us."

Look at your own story and remember an instance of God's deliverance. Rejoice over His deliverance. Give thanks using the words in Psalm 126 by saying, "You have done great things for me, and I will be glad."

GOD'S GIFT OF HOPE

I would have lost heart, unless I had believed
that I would see the goodness of the LORD
in the land of the living.
Wait on the LORD;
be of good courage, and He shall strengthen your heart;
wait, I say, on the LORD!

PSALM 27:13–14

I MARRIED MY OPPOSITE. IT WAS AROUND
the time I turned twenty-two that I realized I was never
going to make any progress on my own. I needed opti-
mism. Just a few months later when I was ordering an
Americano from the coffee shop down the street from
my apartment, my friend introduced me to the new
barista. He was singing cheerfully as he worked, not
caring one bit what anyone thought of it. I thought to
myself, "I guess I'll be marrying that guy." Luckily for

me, he liked the idea, and I am slowly learning from him what it means to live a life of hope.

A life without hope is a life without heart. In Psalm 27:13 David says that he would lose heart if he did not have hope that God was good. Losing heart means losing motivation to live, it means discouragement, it means that life feels pointless and empty. However, if we believe that God is good, and that His goodness comes now to the living, then we will find hope. David says to be patient: "wait on the LORD" (v. 14). Talk to God while you wait on Him; ask for patience, and tell Him you are waiting. You will find in your patience that He strengthens you to have hope. Hope gives us courage and makes us strong in the midst of all sorts of trials.

Earlier in the psalm, David talks about being afraid, but finds comfort in reminding himself that "the LORD is the strength of my life" (v. 1). This acknowledgement gives him the courage to face his enemies without fear. We know from the story of David and Goliath that David was an incredibly brave man, and we see in this psalm that David gained his courage from his unwavering hope.

The world knows the power of hope. Our culture encourages "positive thinking" and "looking for the good" as a way to endure hardship. But it is pointless to have hope unless there is Someone to put hope in. What good is positive thinking unless there is a God who can actually bring about a positive end? The world cannot have the deep hope that Christians have. The hope that David has is a hope that someone will come to his aid, and he knows that the Someone is good and faithful.

The gospel is a story with long periods of waiting, which requires hope from God's people. In Hebrews 11, we are given story after story of God's people who lived their lives waiting, but the hope they had in the midst of their waiting is called faith. Faith that God will come and save, faith that He will rescue us, and faith that He is good are reasons for our hope. Faith and hope feed each other. The greater our faith, the more we will hope, and the more hopeful we are, the more our faith will grow. Being hopeful, believing that everything will have a good outcome, approaching situations in life with a positive attitude, is an act of faith. It is godly to think positively, as long as our hope is based on our belief that God is good and not in our own creative visualization.

When we face troubling financial situations, it is godly to hope and pray that the money we need will come. When we are struggling in a difficult marriage, it is godly to hope and pray that we can both change. When we are sick, it is godly to hope and pray for healing. When we are single, it is godly to hope and pray for a spouse. If we do not have hope, then we will lose heart, which means we will lose courage. Waiting in hope is a sure-fire way to strengthen your faith in God's goodness. Waiting in despair is a great way to lose all your courage. The exhortation to wait on the Lord appears many times in the Psalms. It isn't a fretful, worrisome waiting. It is a waiting that is joined with strength and joy and rejoicing and hope.

Hope is believing that God will be good to you, and finding the comfort of the future in the present. Hope means ignoring any thoughts that things will turn out terribly. Hope means preaching the gospel of God's goodness to yourself. Hope gives strength and joy in the time of waiting. Hope is having courage to believe in the best outcome.

God wants hopeful people. That is why He is constantly telling us in Scripture not to be afraid. God tells us not to be afraid because He knows the outcome. He knows the end of the big story and the little stories, and He says we have reason to hope. In Psalm 71:14–15, David writes, "But I will hope continually, and I will praise You yet more and more. My mouth shall tell of Your righteousness and Your salvation all the day, for I do not know their limits." God's goodness has no limits. There is always hope.

Are there areas in your life where you are afraid things will turn out badly? Do you tell yourself that what you are hoping for will never come? Find courage to keep on hoping for the best by speaking these words to the Lord: "I will hope continually, and I will praise You yet more and more." "I will lose heart, unless I believe that I will see Your goodness." God will make your heart strong in this hope.

HOW TO PRAISE GOD
FOR HIS GOODNESS

Enter into His gates with thanksgiving,
and into His courts with praise.
Be thankful to Him, and bless His name.
For the LORD is good;
His mercy is everlasting,
and His truth endures to all generations.

PSALM 100:4–5

IN C.S. LEWIS'S BOOK *REFLECTIONS ON*
the Psalms, he describes his pre-Christian perception of
a God who demanded praise from His people. He says
that God seemed self-absorbed and arrogant to demand
this. Even after he became a Christian, Lewis struggled
with this idea until he started praising God out of obedience. He then writes, "I did not see that it is in the
process of being worshiped that God communicates His

presence to men."* Once he began to worship God and sing praises to Him, he realized how transformative this is, because it is through praise and thanksgiving that God reveals Himself and gives Himself to us.

Psalm 100 is one of the shortest psalms. The writer exhorts the reader to praise God, to thank Him, to serve Him with gladness. Some of the longer praise psalms list things God has done as reasons to praise Him. Psalm 100 says two things: He made us, and He is good. That by itself should be plenty of reason for us to live lives of praise before Him.

Praise should not just be limited to Sunday worship. Praise is a way of thinking, a way of renewing our minds. Praise gives us something to fill our thoughts with as we work. We can praise God in our thoughts constantly by keeping track of His kindnesses, reminding ourselves of all the things He has done for us and for others, and giving thanks for all the things we see. When our hearts are filled with praise, it will come out in what we say and it will show in our actions. We praise God by telling others of the good things He has done for us, by telling our children the stories of His mercy and kindness to us, by teaching our children to remember those stories and to look for them in their own lives. We praise God by keeping lists of what we are grateful for, and continually reviewing all the good gifts He has given us.

Praise is an act of obedience, but in turn it blesses us. I have heard many healthcare professionals say that rest

* *Reflections on the Psalms* (New York: Harvest/HBJ, 1958), 93.

is the number one thing they prescribe. I believe that praise is for our souls what rest is for our bodies. When our souls are struggling, weary, anxious, fearful, tired, the best remedy is to praise God. Even when life is going well, praise the God who is giving you your life. Make a list of all the things you are thankful for and praise Him for those things. Change your thought patterns throughout your day to come back to that list. Don't feed fearful thoughts to your soul. Fear will poison your soul. Offer praise to God, and He will feed your soul.

I have two daughters, and although they are still young, they are already learning to handle a torrent of emotions. Most of the time, they don't even know why they are feeling a certain way. As we were sitting in the parking lot of the doctor's office, one of my daughters told me that she knew she wasn't supposed to be afraid of going to the doctor, but she just couldn't help the feeling. Her emotions were crippling her from getting out of the car. I told her that if her emotions were getting in the way of obedience, then she needed to ignore them. They were telling her little lies, and she needed to shut them down. Don't think about how you feel, just obey. Then, she needed to pray for the strength to obey. Finally, she needed to fill her heart with a new emotion that would make it easier for her body to obey cheerfully. She needed to give thanks for something, she needed to praise God, which would fill her heart with courage. She needed to fight the fear with praise. We practiced first giving thanks for small things, like the oreos she got at lunch or the sweet girl that played with her at recess. Then we moved on to giving thanks for things that were applicable to the current situation: for all the past doctors' appointments that we had survived, for the free ice cream coupon she would get after the appointment, for the sweet nurse with the kind smile, for doctors that help us get well from illnesses. Before we had even finished the list, we were in and out of the doctor's office and all the feelings had calmed. Praise pushed away fear.

Fighting to trust God with all our minds can be a daily struggle. Praise and thanksgiving are the tools that He has given us to gain the victory over our fears. If we are to love God with all our minds, then our minds have to be trained in praise.

When you are confused, overwhelmed, or afraid, write down all the things you can praise God for. After each item write "Be thankful to Him, and bless His name. For the LORD is good." This act of praise will transform your emotions and fill your prayers with praise.

HOW CREATION BRINGS GOD GLORY

He causes the grass to grow for the cattle,
and vegetation for the service of man,
that he may bring forth food from the earth,
and wine that makes glad the heart of man,
oil to make his face shine,
and bread which strengthens man's heart.
The trees of the LORD are full of sap,
the cedars of Lebanon which He planted,
where the birds make their nests;
the stork has her home in the fir trees.
The high hills are for the wild goats;
the cliffs are a refuge for the rock badgers.

PSALM 104:14–18

PSALM 104 OFFERS PRAISE TO GOD BY surveying His creation. The author walks through a variety of natural phenomena, giving thanks for their majesty. He points out that creation is something God delights in, and He gives creation to us as something for us to delight in. He describes God being always actively part of creation. God delights in bringing things out of the earth that feed and sustain the living things He put on the earth. He delights to watch grass grow, so that it will feed the cows. He delights to see grapes fermenting into wine, so they can make us happy. He delights to make trees sprout branches, so that the birds can build nests in them. He delights to be actively part of the cycle of life in verses 28–30: "You open Your hand, they are filled with good. You hide Your face, they are troubled; You take away their breath, they die and return to their dust. You send forth Your Spirit, they are created; and You renew the face of the earth."

Nothing happens in the earth that God is not actively and thoughtfully involved in, even something so remote as the deepest sea creatures. This should be a great encouragement and joy to us. Our lives are not meaningless; they are a delight to the Lord. He is involved in all of it. When it snows for the fifth day in a row, He is actively involved in blowing the snow down from the cloud. When tulips pop up all over the flower beds in the spring, He is actively involved. This is what Psalm 104 teaches us.

Because God is so actively present in all of creation, our work becomes part of the symphony that He is conducting. When we are driving back and forth to pick children up from school, or planning homeschool field trips, or preparing meals, or balancing a budget, or mowing our lawns, or programming computers, or publishing books, or building homes, we are part of the creation that is dancing before God. Work is a great mercy and blessing. Work gives us the opportunity to become part of creation in a way that delights the Lord and brings glory to Him. Work gives us the opportunity to partake in His joy as He delights in all the inner workings of creation.

Understanding this extends our gratitude for all of creation and for all of our work. If we see another rainstorm in June on the forecast and we fail to be thankful for it, we are failing to delight in what God is actively doing. He makes the clouds His chariots. We should respond with gratitude. If we fail to give thanks for our work, we are failing to take delight in our part of this glorious, mysterious, beautiful world.

Give thanks to God for the work you have today. Take note of all the details of creation giving glory to God through their work, and praise God that you are part of all the glories.

HOW GOD SEES
INGRATITUDE

They soon forgot His works;
they did not wait for His counsel,
but lusted exceedingly in the wilderness,
and tested God in the desert.
And He gave them their request,
but sent leanness into their soul.

PSALM 106:13–15

PSALM 106 IS A HISTORICAL PSALM,
recounting the story of Israel as they left Egypt and wan-
dered in the wilderness. The story is retold here to remember all of God's patience and to praise Him for His
mercy and longsuffering towards the Israelites as they
complained, feared, and failed to trust in the Lord. At
every turn the Israelites failed to show gratitude because
they forgot His works. They were impatient to find their

own way instead of waiting for the Lord to guide them. They told themselves lies about God's goodness, and they believed the lie that He was not going to care for them. They romanticized their memories of Egypt and forgot how powerfully the Lord led them out.

Psalm 106:15 tells us how the Lord responded when the Israelites tested Him so many times with their ingratitude. It says that He gave them what they wanted and sent "leanness to their soul." This is terrifying. Ingratitude is not a sin to take lightly. Ingratitude is a lie to ourselves about God's goodness. When we believe the lie, God makes the lie a reality. He gave them over to their sin, which starved their souls. In 1 Corinthians 10:10–11 Paul speaks of the Israelites saying, "Nor [let us] complain, as some of them also complained, and were destroyed by the destroyer. Now, all these things happened to them as examples, and they were written for our admonition."

Ingratitude is not a sin that we always purposefully commit: it is a state of our heart when we fail to give thanks. This usually begins with self-pity, which leads to envy, which leads to discontent, which leads to a mind-set of ingratitude. If something in our life is not going how we want it to, we can easily slip into self-pity. We can feel sorry for ourselves if we think our work is too stressful, or if others don't show appreciation for us, or if our bodies are in pain, or if our bank account is always low. Even if we are walking through a difficult stage of life, we should not give in to selfishly thinking that we deserve more. This kind of thinking leads us to compare our lives to others' lives. It leads us to cast glances off to the side to see how everyone else is doing. When everyone else seems to be doing better than we are, we wallow in our self-pity and envy. We know that envy is rottenness to the bones (Proverbs 14:30). Envy is the foundation of discontentment. When we focus on others who are living disease-free, wealthy, stress-free lives, we find our life to be wanting. We become discontent with the story we have been given, and we stop giving thanks for it. When we are not giving thanks, God gives us over to our ingratitude. He lets us live the horrible life that we think we already have. We become blind and we stop seeing His mercy and His goodness. Gratitude is what will heal the blindness.

We have to fight an active war in our minds every day. The sins of self-pity and envy begin when we are not in control of our thoughts. God cares about what is going through our heads every day. He commanded us to love Him with our minds. How can we do that while entertaining thoughts of self-pity and envy? If there are thoughts in our minds that are not thankful, that are not focused on His goodness, that are not remembering His constant mercy, then they are sinful and have no place in us.

Gratitude is the strongest weapon for the war of our minds. Giving thanks for all the past events, giving thanks for whatever we see in front of us, giving thanks because we know who holds the future, will crowd out self-pity. At the end of Psalm 106, the psalmist praises God because even though the Israelites failed to love God, He was still merciful to them. He was capable of forgiving the worship of the golden calf. If we have fallen into self-pity, envy, discontent, and ingratitude, there is hope in forgiveness. Being forgiven is a sweet gift that starts us on the road of gratitude for all things—for the piles of dishes, for the people tramping mud through the kitchen, for the work in front of us, for the annoying coworkers, for the undiagnosed illnesses, for the teething babies. Give thanks for the hard things and the good gifts—for the paychecks, for health and energy, for plenty of food, for tiny heartbeats on an ultrasound. Gratitude gives us power to see clearly that God is in all of this and to keep our minds focused on His goodness.

Recall a time when God has been kind to you despite your ingratitude. As the writer of Psalm 106 does, thank God for the mercy He showed you then.

GOD'S GENERATIONAL PROMISES

Walk about Zion,
and go all around her.
Count her towers;
mark well her bulwarks;
consider her palaces;
that you may tell it to the generation following.
For this is God, our God forever and ever;
He will be our guide even to death.

PSALM 48:12–14

PSALM 48 IS WRITTEN BY THE SONS OF Korah and is a song of praise about the greatness of Zion. The greatness is a result of God's presence. He has chosen Zion and He has blessed her. The instruction in verse 13 is to observe how great and beautiful and strong the city is in order to teach the next generation.

There are several places in the Psalms that talk about
God being faithful to the generations:

> The counsel of the LORD stands forever, the plans of
> His heart to all generations. (Ps. 33:11)

> They shall fear You as long as the sun and moon
> endure, throughout all generations. (Ps. 72:5)

> For the LORD is good; His mercy is everlasting, and
> His truth endures to all generations. (Ps. 100:5)

God loves to bless generationally. He loves to keep
His promises to families. It is extremely important that
we think this way also. Being in Christ is not only about
individual piety; it is also about being part of the large
body of the Church. It is about seeing that the next generation knows that God is good. We have to count all
the towers and bulwarks and palaces, all the ways that
God has been our strength and refuge and protector and
provider, and recount them to our children. Those blessings, that strength and refuge and provision, is for them
too. These encouragements are not only for biological
parents of children; they are also for believers that do
not have children. We are all part of the body of Christ,
and we are all responsible to tell the next generation
about the goodness of God. Even if you do not have any
children of your own, you should be counting and recounting the ways that God has been your strength and

your protector. Speaking as a parent of three, I see great results in the faith of my children when what I teach them about God is reiterated by school teachers, aunts, uncles, Sunday School teachers, soccer coaches, and ballet teachers. Find a place where you can connect with and encourage children to see God's goodness. They need your help.

One of the best parenting tips I was given was to treat my children like Christians. Believe that they are part of the covenant with God, that they are part of the Church, part of Zion. Baptize them, give them bread and wine, teach them to memorize Scripture. Read the Psalms to them and tell them that all those promises are theirs. Take them to church with you and help them sit through the long sermons until they start to understand. Sing hymns to them because those will be their comforts; those belong to them. Teach them to sing, teach them to read, teach them to keep prayer journals and gratitude books. Teach them to live as followers of Christ because you believe that they already belong to Christ. Do not wait until they show an interest. Make Christianity their life and breath before they even know they need to breathe.

You will find that there will be times when your children's struggle with sin is strong, and they don't seem to be acting much like Christians. You may start to believe that they are not Christians, or even if you don't admit that, you may start to treat them as though they are not Christians. When a seven-year-old is struggling with lying, it is easy for parents to treat their child like they are a liar all the time. When a teenager is struggling with disrespecting his mother, it is easy to think of him as a disrespectful son. Instead of treating our children like they are the sin, we need to come alongside them and help them fight the sin. Give them the tools they need to fight. Give them discipline, give them Scripture, give them love. If you do not, they will start to believe that they are liars or disrespectful or haters or biters or uncontrollable. Fight with them against the sin; don't leave them in the sin to fight against you. This will only cause them to doubt their faith and to doubt that the Holy Spirit is in them. If we truly believe that our children are Christians, then we will treat them like they are. All our discipline and correction will stem from a desire to help them. Your faith that the Spirit is in them gives them faith. Teach them to praise God for never leaving them alone in their sin, and for always guiding them. Pray prayers of gratitude with your children. Show them how to thank God for all His faithfulness to past saints, and to praise Him for His faithfulness now.

The next time you are faced with a challenge in parenting, recount to your children the good things God has done for you. Praise God with your children and remind them that "this is God, our God forever and ever; He will be our guide even to death."

PRAISING GOD FOR HIS LOVINGKINDNESS

O God, You are my God;
early will I seek You;
my soul thirsts for You;
my flesh longs for You
in a dry and thirsty land where there is no water.
So I have looked for You in the sanctuary,
to see Your power and Your glory.
Because Your lovingkindness is better than life,
my lips shall praise You.

PSALM 63:1–3

MANY TIMES IN SCRIPTURE, LOVINGKINDNESS is used to describe God's character. In Psalm 63 David even goes so far to say that God's lovingkindness is better than life! David wrote this psalm while he was trapped in the wilderness. He was in a situation where he easily could have lost his life, but he says that God's love is sweeter to him than keeping it. In the midst of his terrifying trial, he seeks after God with all his heart. He says that he is thirsty for God. He is desperate to be in fellowship with God, and he praises God for His lovingkindness.

God's lovingkindness is often used to describe the kind of covenantal relationship that God has with His people. In the first commandment God says,

> Thou shalt not bow down thyself unto them, nor serve them; for I Jehovah thy God am a jealous God, visiting the iniquity of the fathers upon the children, upon the third and upon the fourth generation of them that hate me, and showing lovingkindness unto thousands of them that love me and keep my commandments. (Ex. 20:5–6, ASV)

When Solomon prayed in 1 Kings 3:6, he spoke of God's lovingkindness towards David:

> And Solomon said, Thou hast showed unto thy servant David my father great lovingkindness, according as he walked before thee in truth, and in righteousness, and in uprightness of heart with thee; and thou hast kept for him this great lovingkindness, that thou hast given him a son to sit on his throne, as it is this day. (ASV)

God's covenant relationship with His people is defined by His lovingkindness. It is His promise that He will show towards generations. David shows us in Psalm 63 that the remembrance of this promise fills his thirsting soul with praise.

Webster's dictionary defines lovingkindness as "tender and benevolent affection." God's love for us is sweet, gentle, and generous. We often think that being a Christian means we are willing to follow a specific lifestyle. But this is not the faith that we see throughout the Psalms. David shows us that belonging to God means we know His lovingkindness, and we love Him in return. The Christian lifestyle will flow from our love. When we believe that we are loved by a kind God, we want to follow His law. As the psalmist says in Psalm 119:97, "Oh, how I love Your law! It is my meditation all the day." This is written by a man who would rather die than lose God's affection towards him.

If following God's law is a natural ramification of loving God, then we first have to accept His love. Believing that we are loved by God is one of the greatest hurdles in the life of a Christian. The older I get, the more of my own sin I see, which makes God's love even more unbelievable. Our sinful nature wants to convince us that God does not love us. When we doubt God's love for us, the only solution is to run toward Him, to praise Him for His lovingkindness, and to look at His power and glory. David shows us how to accept God's love by offering praise. But praise here does not mean that we only express gratitude for the things God has already given to us. Praising God like David means that we chase after Him so that we may receive more of His affection. If we believe God loves us, then we know that following after Him will reveal more of His love. We seek after Him like a thirsty man in the wilderness seeks after water. We are vigilant to find times that we can read the Word; we are disciplined to attend worship; we are constantly seeking Him in prayer throughout our day. In verse eight, David says, "My soul follows close behind You." When David chases after God, doubt is pushed out of his soul. When he praises God, his heart and his soul get in line with the truth.

Praise God for His love for you and chase after Him with these words: "O God, You are my God; early will I seek You; my soul thirsts for You; my flesh longs for You in a dry and thirsty land where there is no water. So I have looked for You in the sanctuary, to see Your power and Your glory. Because Your lovingkindness is better than life, my lips shall praise You."

GOD'S GIFT OF
COMFORT

You, who have shown me great and severe troubles,
shall revive me again,
and bring me up again from the depths of the earth.
You shall increase my greatness,
and comfort me on every side.

PSALM 71:20–21

PSALM 71 WAS WRITTEN BY AN OLD MAN as he struggled with fear that his old age would bring weakness which would make him vulnerable to his enemies. In spite of his concern, he praises God. He knows he can find comfort and hope in God. He knows that God will protect and deliver him. David pours out his concern to God and finds comfort in remembering the character of God's faithfulness to him throughout all the previous years.

Throughout Scripture God promises to comfort us. In 2 Corinthians 1:3, Paul calls Him "the Father of mercies and God of all comfort." Isaiah speaks frequently of God as a comforter, one example being Isaiah 49:13: "For the LORD has comforted His people, and will have mercy on His afflicted." David knew God was a comforter. Because of his many trials, he found solace in God many times. In Psalm 71, he specifically talks about God being a "comfort on every side" (verse 21). He is completely submerged in God's consolation. He does not have a fear that is not met with equal comfort.

David knows how to find this comfort in God: he praises Him. He remembers the past deliverances when God brought him up "again from the depths of the earth" (verse 20). It is his recollection of God's goodness that brings him comfort in his present circumstances. Recalling God's goodness is an act of praise towards Him. Philippians 4:6–7 says something similar: "Be anxious for nothing, but in everything by prayer and supplication, with thanksgiving, let your requests be made known to God; and the peace of God, which surpasses all understanding, will guard your hearts and minds through Christ Jesus." In order to find peace, we have to make our requests known with thanksgiving. Thanksgiving is a form of praise. Remembering God's mercy leads us to find comfort.

There are some circumstances when it can be difficult to find mercy. Some situations are so tangled and dark that our cries to God don't include much thanksgiving.

When we find it hard to praise God in the midst of a trial, David gives us a reminder of what we can be thankful for. He says "you shall increase my greatness" (verse 21). David knows that God will use his difficulty to mold him and create something great out of it, even when there is no light at the end of the tunnel. God's path through trial always leads to greatness. If you are struggling to find something within your situation to be thankful for, give thanks for what will come out of it. Praise God for the strength He is shaping in you. Praise Him for the future.

A couple of years ago I was given a medication by a naturopathic doctor that made me very sick. I quit the medication as soon as I realized what was causing the illness, but my symptoms did not completely subside. I continued to struggle with daily nausea, debilitating migraines, fatigue, and insomnia for almost a year. Fears and frustration were a constant enemy. I remember watching the snow fall one particular afternoon. I wanted to take my kids sledding, but I knew the piercing migraine would keep us at home. Instead of giving in to the self-pity, I found great comfort in knowing that God would bring me out of this darkness into something great, that I would be more Christ-like after this trial than I was going into it. I recounted to God all the ways that He had brought me out of hardships before, and I thanked Him for all the fruit that came from those hardships. I thanked Him for all the times He had asked me to die but brought me up from death into a greater life. I found, as David did, that praising God for His promise of greatness comforted me "on every side." I was comforted in the midst of my struggle, and I was comforted in the outcome.

God's comforts always enable us to become something new. 2 Corinthians 1:3–4 says, "Blessed be the God and Father of our Lord Jesus Christ, the Father of mercies and God of all comfort, who comforts us in all our tribulation, that we may be able to comfort those who are in any trouble, with the comfort with which we ourselves are comforted by God." His comforts make us vessels of comfort. His comfort makes us strong enough to give. His healing sends us out to become great healers.

Recall how God has lifted you up out of many trials. Praise Him for those times: "You, who have shown me great and severe troubles, shall revive me again, and bring me up again from the depths of the earth." Find comfort in knowing that God will lift you out of your current struggles, calling you to become something greater, calling you to be a comforter: "You shall increase my greatness, and comfort me on every side."

PRAISING GOD
FOR TRIALS

Oh, bless our God, you peoples!
And make the voice of His praise to be heard,
Who keeps our soul among the living,
and does not allow our feet to be moved.
For You, O God, have tested us;
You have refined us as silver is refined.
You brought us into the net;
You laid affliction on our backs.
You have caused men to ride over our heads;
we went through fire and through water;
but You brought us out to rich fulfillment.

PSALM 66:8–12

PSALM 66 OFFERS PRAISE TO GOD FOR HIS
wonderful works and thanks Him for what He has done.
However, it is not written because the author has never
faced suffering. We see in verses eight through twelve

that he has seen affliction, and it is because of the affliction that he praises God even more. He sees God's hand
in the affliction, and he views the affliction as a mercy
because of how it refined him. Just as in Psalm 71, we
see here that believing in a positive outcome will bring
gratitude for the hardship.

Martin Luther once said, "It is the way of God: he
humbles that he might exalt, he kills that he might make
alive, he confounds that he might glorify."* God always
uses suffering so that He might exalt us even more. This
is the message of the book of James. We should rejoice
when we face trials because God is using them to make
us grow in patience and righteousness, which James says
will make us perfect and complete, lacking in nothing
(James 1:4). God uses trials to refine us, to burn away
all the sinful habits, to make us complete. The psalmist
here says that they were brought through "fire and water," but on the other side there was "rich fulfillment."
God does not allow trials to come into our lives unless
He plans to use them to refine us.

This is a very easy thing to say, but a very hard thing
to live. It is easy for us to say that God is using our trials
for good, but it is very hard to live this way when we are
right in the middle of the struggle. When we are really
suffering, we are constantly looking for answers to re-
move the suffering. We often obsess over the suffering
by thinking or talking about it constantly. We allow the
suffering to take our joy and our peace. We know that

* Quoted in Burroughs, *The Rare Jewel of Christian Contentment*, 67.

God is using the suffering for our good in the long run, but it is easy to lose sight of how that changes our view of the suffering while it is happening.

James says that in the middle of suffering, we should rejoice because we know that the long end of it is blessing. He says that we should have the mindset of welcoming trial, because we believe so strongly in God's ability to glorify us through it. But what does this look like? How can we welcome a miscarriage? How can we welcome a chronic illness in our child? How can we welcome infertility?

The first step is to offer praise in the middle of the suffering even when we don't feel like it or see any good. Giving thanks for the trial is an act of faith, faith in what we cannot see yet. Giving thanks says that we believe God has a plan for our benefit in this trial and that we believe He will be faithful to His promises to make us perfect through tribulation.

Another thing we can do while in the middle of a trial is cultivate patience. Do not be in a such a hurry to figure out the solution or to make the trial go away. We should pray for deliverance, and we should seek help when necessary. But we must always understand that the Lord will allow our suffering to go on as long as is necessary for our refinement, not one day less and not one day more. He is overseeing all of it. We can rest in the trial because we believe that it is part of His work in us. My husband is fond of quoting Psalm 23:5 when he reminds me to rest in the middle of a trial: "You prepare a table before me in the presence of my enemies." We do not have to strive impatiently to eradicate all trials from our lives. We have to trust God to determine what our deliverance will look like. Maybe our deliverance will be an eradication of our problem; maybe our deliverance will be a table of feasting set before us in the midst of our problem. We need to rest in the promise of rich fulfillment.

The third thing we can do to praise God in a trial is to submit to His plan. James reminds us of this in James 4:6: "God resists the proud, but gives grace to the humble." Humble yourself. Admit to God that you need refinement. Look for what He is changing in you with this trial. Become a student of the lesson He is teaching you. When He tears down your idols, go in with a sledgehammer and help Him. Let go of the sin He is burning off. He is using your trial as a training tool, so look for the strengthening in your life that is a result of this training.

As you walk through hardships, praise God with these words: "You laid affliction on our backs. You have caused men to ride over our heads; we went through fire and through water; but You brought us out to rich fulfillment." Recount to God all the times He has brought you out of fire.

PRAISING GOD IN FAILURE

You have turned for me my mourning into dancing;
You have put off my sackcloth and clothed me with gladness,
to the end that my glory may sing praise to You
and not be silent.
O LORD my God, I will give thanks to You forever.
PSALM 30:11–12

THE GOSPEL IS A STORY OF GOD USING brokenness to create glory. He uses a cross to save the world through His Son. He uses Paul, a man who persecuted Christians, to write a large portion of the Bible. In all His stories, God is constantly taking crookedness and making it straight. He takes weak things to confound the wise. He turns ashes into gladness, and failures into glories. He often creates good out of evil, and in Psalm 30 David praises God that He has turned mourning into dancing. He has turned something devastating into something joyous.

We do not often know what God is doing in our stories, which is why we need to keep this praise at the forefront of our minds. We need to keep singing, "You have turned for me my mourning into dancing," because you know that in the past He has and in the future He will. He will turn the pain and suffering you currently experience into gladness for you. We often don't understand how He will do this. We can't see how it is possible for Him to turn our greatest hurts into our greatest strengths, but we have to believe that it is His way.

In his book *Contentment*, Robert Swenson says,

> Do we know enough to label something a failure? We should never call anything a failure until God has spoken. We dare not label our work, our lives, our kids, our churches, or our world as failure until God pounds the gavel. Massive surprises await us, perhaps in this life, surely in the next.*

We can easily look at small struggling churches, or wayward teens, or dead-end jobs and call them failures. We can see all the things that are not righteous about them, and we can either stand in judgment of others or in judgment of ourselves because we see something that looks crooked. But we should not forget that even in the darkest parts of our stories, and in the dark parts

* Swenson, *Contentment*, Kindle loc. 230.

of others' stories, God is able and willing to make the rough places plain. He is looking at things that seem like failures, knowing that He will use the "failure" to redeem and strengthen.

We cannot even comprehend the extent of God's goodness. We can see the daily kindnesses that He shows us, but we cannot see all He is doing. When we praise God, we show Him that we have faith in the goodness that we can't see. Hebrews 11:1 tells us that faith is the substance of things hoped for. Our praise tells God that we have faith. Faith in God's goodness brings His goodness into focus so we can see it. Even if we have things in our life that we think are failures, God sees them as opportunities to show us His goodness.

Do you see failures in your life? Or do you have a hardship in your past that still stings? Start looking for all the ways He has used it to change you, to refine you, to strengthen your faith. List all the idols He has torn down with this hardship. Even after you have found dozens of good things that have come from your trial, you still have no idea how great the glory will be that He is creating out of it. He is the God who takes darkness and makes the world, who takes the grave and makes it the door to life. He will take all your sackcloth and turn it into gladness.

When Miriam stood on the other side of the Red Sea, she took a timbrel in her hand, and she started singing. Moments earlier she and all her people had been at death's door, sandwiched between the sea and Pharaoh's army. The Israelites pointed to Moses and called him a failure. They called their decision to follow him a failure. God took a situation that seemed so dire, so dark, so hopeless, and made it a glorious triumph for His people. He hasn't changed. It is the same God that you pray to today. Our prayers of praise show that we believe it, and looking into the face of our hardships we can sing with Miriam, "The horse and its rider has He thrown into the sea" (Ex. 15:21).

When your failures crush your spirit, remember the God who is writing your story. He is the One who makes glory from those failures. Praise Him by praying these words: "You have turned for me my mourning into dancing; You have put off my sackcloth and clothed me with gladness, to the end that my glory may sing praise to You and not be silent. O LORD my God, I will give thanks to You forever."

PART III

PREACHING *the* PSALMS *to* YOURSELF

INTRODUCTION

PSALMS OF PREACHING ARE PASSAGES that declare an encouraging truth about God. In this section I will show you how to take these truths and preach them to yourself. In Philippians 4:8 Paul writes, "Finally, brethren, whatever things are true, whatever things are noble, whatever things are just, whatever things are pure, whatever things are lovely, whatever things are of good report, if there is any virtue and if there is anything praiseworthy, meditate on these things." But how do we know what is true and noble and just and pure? The Psalms tell us. Psalm 3 tells us that God is our shield. This is a lovely truth that we should let our minds rest on. Affirming that God is our shield and dwelling on it strengthens our faith to believe it is true.

In the Psalms we frequently see the psalmist speaking to his own soul. Psalm 43:5 says, "Why are you cast down, O my soul? And why are you disquieted within me? Hope in God!" The psalmist is struggling to rejoice. He knows in his mind that God loves him, but he does not feel it in his soul. So he preaches truth to himself. He tells his soul to hope in God. He reminds his soul of the good things God has done and who God is. In these passages, we will learn to speak to our own hearts. We will look at truths found in the Psalms and I will challenge you to use them as soul fuel when you face struggles in life.

It is a well-known fact that the average human has thousands of thoughts pass through his mind every day. Paul understood in his exhortation to the Philippians that those thoughts have the power to build or destroy our faith, which is why he gave the Philippians a list of things to think about. Loving God with all our minds means that we bring even our thoughts under His lordship. The Psalms will give you practical examples of what thoughts are glorifying to God.

I often wake in the morning with a singular thought running through my mind, and frequently that thought is a verse from Scripture. My mind is simple in the morning, not crowded yet by the cares and conversations of the day. The Spirit often meets me there and gives me the Scripture I will need for that day, but I have to put the Scripture into my mind for the Spirit to use it for my encouragement. Your body is a temple of the Holy Spirit (1 Cor. 6:19). He lives in you. If you put the food of Scripture into your body, the Spirit is there to nourish you with it when you are hungry. So feed on the Psalms, preach them to your soul throughout your day, and the Spirit will use them to strengthen you when you need it the most.

GOD'S PERSPECTIVE
OF MAN

He fashions their hearts individually;
He considers all their works.

PSALM 33:15

PSALM 33 BEGINS WITH PRAISE, WITH declaring that "the earth is full of the goodness of the LORD" (verse 5). Then the author describes how the Lord created the earth and how He continues to interact with it, making sure that the plans of the "nations" do not prosper. It concludes by reminding us that He is watching out for those who hope in Him, and He is readily waiting to be our help and our shield. It is a psalm of encouragement and comfort. Verses 13–15 are particularly powerful. They paint a picture of God looking down from heaven at the beautiful earth He created and working with us as individual people to guide our hearts, our decisions, and our work. Seeing the world through this perspective protects us from two things: feeling like we are worthless, and being envious of others.

It can often feel like our particular works go unnoticed, because many of them do go unnoticed by people. God sees what is happening in secret. He sees all the diaper changes that you are doing with a cheerful heart, He sees all the little sacrifices you make in your budget so you can provide an education for your children, He sees all the hidden self-control that you exercise that others do not see. But it isn't just that He sees. He also plans those things. He fashions each of our hearts to go in the direction that He has for us. He creates each of our stories. He puts particular people in your story just for you. He puts a particular amount of money in your bank account. He puts you in a particular city, in a particular year in history, in a particular job for a reason. He isn't ignoring any of the details. He is using you to bring glory.

As we seek to build Christian communities in churches or schools or cities, one of the most poisonous sins we will encounter is envy. Envy will rot friendships, destroy good leaders, and tear down beneficial work. We can build nothing if envy is pervasive. Psalm 33 paints a picture of God working through each of our lives in separate ways to accomplish good, but envy doesn't look through the eyes of Psalm 33. Envy forgets that God intends different people for different things. Envy makes people think they are more important than God's plan for them. Envy corrodes contentment and joy. It begins even in small children, wishing they had all the toys their friends have. The terrifying thing about envy is that people do not mature out of envy. The older you grow, the greater your envy will grow if you do not confess and turn from it. In adults, envy often masks itself as dislike. We don't like a lady at church because she is always talking about her beautiful house, but in reality we are the ones who are envious of her faithfulness and care for her home. We don't like our boss because our hearts are envious that he has higher paychecks and longer vacations. Any time we are tempted to be critical of something that is not a sin, we should examine our hearts for envy.

God makes us all differently and gives us to each other as gifts to sharpen one another. If our hearts are full of envy, sharpening cannot happen. We have to see how God sees. If we see another person strong in an area where we are weak, we can look to learn from them. If we see another person weak where we are strong, we can help them in a kind and uncritical way. He makes some of us to be feet, some to be hands, some to be eyes. Paul tells us this in 1 Corinthians 12. Feet should be the best feet they can be, and eyes should be the best eyes they can be, and the two together can make a body walk in the right direction. Remind yourself of God's individual love for the person He created you to be. Preach this truth to yourself—that He is fashioning your heart and creating a good work in you.

*Do you struggle to feel confident in the roles God has placed
you in? Do you struggle with envy? Find contentment in your
own story by affirming this truth: "He fashions your heart
individually; He considers all your works."*

GOD AS THE HEALER

Bless the LORD, O my soul;
and all that is within me, bless His holy name!
Bless the LORD, O my soul,
and forget not all His benefits:
Who forgives all your iniquities,
Who heals all your diseases.

PSALM 103:1–3

I LOVE PSALM 103. IT IS A SONG OF PRAISE written by David. He commands his soul to bless the Lord, to give thanks to the Lord, to praise the Lord for all the different ways that He has been good. David praises God for His mercy and forgiveness of sins, for His kindness, for His patience, for His endurance, and for His healing.

God cares very much about our bodies. They are His handiwork. He cares if we are in physical pain and discomfort. In fact, forgiveness of sins and healing often go hand in hand in Scripture. This is because sickness is a visible result of Fall. Jesus came to take away both the sickness and the sin. When He heals the paralytic in Matthew 9, He first forgives his sins. Since the doubtful people standing by cannot see with their eyes that sins are forgiven, Jesus shows them a visible sign by healing the man's legs. Many of the things that David praises God for in Psalm 103 are spiritual, but God's care of our health is a kindness that others who have little faith can see. Jesus came to earth with His eyes peeled for the sick. He was searching for them, looking for opportunities to restore bodies to full health. Healing was the perfect visible sample of the kind of healing that God does in our hearts.

We live in a fascinating time of medical advances. Our knowledge of nutrition is better than it has been for centuries, which results in some naturopaths believing that everything can be healed with the correct diet. On the other end of the spectrum, conventional medical science has made huge progress in the last century, and primary care doctors have the ability to prevent and treat more diseases than ever before. Within each of these schools of thought, there is a lie that knowledge is our answer. Our current medical advances can tempt us to have faith in the knowledge. As Christians, we should always remember that God is the healer. He often uses healthy diets and modern medicine as a means to heal, but healing belongs to Him. Healing is His tool to show His forgiving power in a tangible way.

As a mother and wife, I spend much time caring for the health of my family. I research the healthiest foods that fit within our budget. I spend time planning, shopping, and preparing those foods. I have to make sure the little ones actually eat at meal time. When my children are sick, I care for them. I take them in for regular dentist and doctor checkups. Much of my job in the family is overseeing their health and my health. It is hard work, and I know that it is futile work without the blessing and healing of the Lord. I plant the seeds of good health to the best of my ability, but the crop is in the Lord's hands. Trusting in God is more important than cod liver oil.

At some point, physical harm will end our life, whether by trauma, disease, or old age. David reminds us of this in verse 15 of Psalm 103, when he points out that man is like the fading grass. The mercy of the Lord stands forever. Sickness is not something that we can escape, but mercy and forgiveness will rescue our souls. Even when our final disease or trauma takes our life, God will be standing there with healing, because God will be standing there with mercy.

Have you sought healing for yourself or others? In all your seeking, acknowledge the Lord as the true healer. Pray the words of Psalm 103. Admonish your soul to bless the Lord "Who forgives all your iniquities, who heals all your diseases." Preach this truth to yourself. If you believe He has the power to forgive your sins, how much more does He have the power to heal your body?

GOD AS A SHIELD

LORD, how they have increased who trouble me!
Many are they who rise up against me.
Many are they who say of me,
"There is no help for him in God." *Selah*
But You, O LORD, are a shield for me,
my glory and the One who lifts up my head.
PSALM 3:1–3

DO YOU EVER FEEL LIKE ARROWS ARE FLYING?
I don't think I really knew what it was like to feel temptations coming at me like arrows until I became a mother
of multiple children. I had often experienced a temptation to sin of course, but I didn't know what it was like to
feel so many temptations coming at a rapid pace. Sometimes everyone is whining for different things, the littlest
one is doing something dangerous across the room, and
I can't get to him because I am helping another child,
dinner is burning on the stove, and my phone is ringing.

There are afternoons where I correct the same child for the same thing over and over again with barely fifteen minutes in between. The temptations to be impatient, to be unkind, to complain, to correct my child harshly, to self-pity, to be angry, to lose control are like arrows zipping towards me. This is, of course, not the only time when temptations fly. A teenage girl can find social events to be petri dishes for envy, a young man can be constantly confronted with the temptation to lust, someone with chronic pain can find that they are constantly tempted to discontent, or a parent of a sick child can struggle with continual worry.

All these temptations to sin have one thing in common: they all say, "There is no help in God," just as the psalmist describes in Psalm 3. When Christ hung on the cross, there were men literally standing beneath Him mocking His hope in God. If God was a shield for Him then, how much more will He be a shield for us now? When a mother falls into self-pity, she is essentially believing the lie that God is not there to help, that He is not going to continually fill her with more strength to continually give. When a young woman falls into envy, she is believing that there is no help in God, that He has not been generous and kind to purposefully give her exactly what she has. That is why we need a shield. We need God to be our shield, to keep us safe from the arrows of temptation that want us to believe that there is no hope in Him.

There are many moments when I pray beneath my breath, "You, O LORD, are a shield for me. Protect me in this moment." When I have been up all night with a baby and the toddler has taken on a new love of decorating the walls with markers, God is my shield, my shield against anger and impatience. When unexpected expenses have been extreme and the mortgage is due, He is my shield, my shield from fear and worry. When I am surrounded by women who have accomplished more than I have in their homes or their jobs, He is my shield, my shield against envy and discontent. I have asked Him thousands of times to be my shield, and He has never failed to protect me.

In Psalm 3, God is not only called "a shield." He is also called "the One who lifts up my head." Lifting up a head can refer to a rise in status and power. After God protects us, He glorifies us. Just as He made Jesus king over His enemies, God makes us kings over the temptations that surround us.

Lifting up our head can also refer to the literal action of going from having a bowed head to a lifted head— from a humble place to a regal place. Like a parent who lifts their crying child's chin to tell them words of hope, God gives us hope to lift our heads. Have you ever been in prayer, pleading with God, and finding Him to be your only comfort when your story is full of temptations to despair? How can you rise up and step back into normal life when normal life is too much? God is the One who will end your pleading. He is the One who provides answers.

Jesus often told people to get up. In Matthew 9:6, when Jesus meets the paralytic, He tells him, "Arise! Take up your bed, and go to your home." Later in the same chapter, He took the ruler's dead daughter by the hand and she "arose." After the transfiguration, the disciples who witnessed it immediately fell on their faces, and Jesus told them to "arise, and do not be afraid." God is in the business of getting people up, onto their feet, off their faces, and only He can do this because He is their hope. When we are struggling and we come to God in prayer, His protection and the hope we find in Him are what get us up off our knees and back to work with a shield around us.

Do you have arrows of temptation flying towards you? Are you discouraged by these struggles? Find strength to persevere by affirming the words of Psalm 3, "You, O Lord, are a shield for me, my glory and the One who lifts up my head." Preach to your heart that you have a shield who will not allow you to be harmed.

GOD'S FAVOR
AS PROTECTION

But let all those rejoice who put their trust in You;
let them ever shout for joy, because You defend them;
Let those also who love Your name
Be joyful in You.
For You, O LORD, will bless the righteous;
with favor You will surround him as with a shield.

PSALM 5:11–12

ALTHOUGH WE KNOW THAT GOD IS OUR protector, it can be hard to resist temptation. I think many of us still feel very weak, especially when we are struggling with an ongoing, besetting sin. We know that God is mighty enough to protect us, to give us a way of escape, but sometimes we still fall, and that can be so discouraging. In the previous chapter, we learned that God has promised to be a shield around us. But in Psalm

5, David tells us how God does this. He compares God's favor to a shield. It is God's love and approval that surround us and gives us the strength to resist sin.

If you have spent time training children, you know that they obey much more readily when they are secure in your love for them. When they know that you approve of them and love them, they want to please you by being obedient, and their guilt in disobedience is unbearable to them because they have let you down. Our obedience to God is like this. We are much more able to resist temptation and follow God when we are convinced of His love. When we believe in our hearts that He rejoices over us, when we believe that He delights in us, then we do not want to displease Him. The assurance of His love becomes a protection against sin.

How has God blessed you? What things do you see in your life that assure you that He is caring for you? Give thanks for those things. You will start to see how abundant His love is even in the details. Do you read Scripture regularly to remind yourself of what Christ has done, to remind yourself of the love He has for you specifically? Read it, highlight it, memorize it. Get in a pulpit in your mind and preach it to yourself. Pour yourself into God's Word as though it were a story written for you, because it is. Let the knowledge of how much He approves of you sink in, and His love, His favor, will surround you like a shield.

Isaiah 62:5 says, "And as the bridegroom rejoices over the bride, so shall your God rejoice over you," and

Zephaniah 3:17, "The Lord your God in your midst, the Mighty One, will save; He will rejoice over you with gladness, He will quiet you with His love, He will rejoice over you with singing." This is how God sees His faithful remnant in Israel: He rejoices over the people who follow Him. He rejoices over us now. He rejoices over our work and our faithful families and our weekly worship and our daily prayers and our hobbies and our creations and our acts of kindness towards one another. He is a kind Father who finds great delight in the seemingly meaningless details of our lives. I have come to a greater understanding of this as I interact with my own children. Before I was a mother, I was very particular about what was displayed in my home. I wanted it to be simple and minimalistic. But now when my three-year-old son draws a dot on a page and calls it a spider, I find myself busting out the Scotch tape and looking for an empty space on the fridge. I can't help but rejoice over any small thing that he does because my love for him is so great.

When we are struggling to resist sin, it can be easy to think that we need to conjure up more self-control from ourselves. But the Psalms teach us that the real protection from our enemies comes when we are secure in God's love towards us. He does all the work of protecting. When we stumble, He has even offered us His own Son's life to give us a way to be made right again. When we are forgiven, we are made strong so that we can resist next time. Our sins are erased. We do not identify with them any longer. You are new. His forgiveness makes you a new person.

List some of the ways that God has shown you His love. Let His love become a protection for you by seeing that you are safe, you are approved of, you are forgiven. Praise the Lord for this love by praying these words: "For You, O LORD, will bless the righteous; with favor You will surround him as with a shield."

MEDITATING ON GOD'S GOODNESS

The lines have fallen to me in pleasant places;
yes, I have a good inheritance.
I will bless the LORD who has given me counsel;
my heart also instructs me in the night seasons.
I have set the LORD always before me;
because He is at my right hand I shall not be moved.
Therefore my heart is glad, and my glory rejoices;
my flesh also will rest in hope.
For You will not leave my soul in Sheol,
nor will You allow Your Holy One to see corruption.
You will show me the path of life;
in Your presence is fullness of joy;
at Your right hand are pleasures forevermore.

PSALM 16:6–11

THIS IS ONE OF MY FAVORITE PASSAGES IN Scripture. It is a confession of gratitude and full of hope.

It doesn't just tell of the goodness of God: it tells how extensive it is. God's goodness extends to all the past, all the present, and all the future.

David looks over his life, and despite the multitude of trials that he was brought through, he says that the lines have fallen in pleasant places. He is content. He is thankful. He says that the Lord has guided him and shown his heart what to do. In Psalm 63, David speaks about meditating on his bed at night, and here we see that the Lord is guiding his heart through those nights of prayer. The Lord is showing David what he should do, and he becomes confident in his decisions. David preaches to himself the truth that God is guiding his meditation. He says that even in death God will save him: his soul will not see corruption. Finally, he will be in the presence of God, experiencing fullness of joy and pleasures forever. David is looking back over his life and he says he is content with how things have gone. He is confident with how things are going. He is strong to face the future.

This is one of the clearer places that we see the Psalms talking about Jesus. In verse ten, when it says that the "Holy One" will not see corruption, that is a direct description of Christ not being allowed to stay in the grave. He was not dead long enough for His body to decay. Christ's life was as the rest of this passage describes. God cared for Him every step of the way, providing a good father and mother to raise Him, providing friends and disciples to travel with Him, providing food and places to rest and even tax money when He needed it. Jesus could look at His life and echo the words of David. He had contentment and strength and wisdom and confidence and direction. And at the very last, He was offered a place at God's right hand.

The Incarnation gives us all these things. Because Christ took on flesh, we are partakers in His life and death and resurrection. Just like Christ, we have guidance from the Father through our lives, and God will not leave our souls to see corruption. This is the story we get to live. We are given a story of mercy from start to finish. The Lord will draw our lines in pleasant places. He will show us kindness. Even in trials, He will guide our hearts. When we keep Him before us, we are strong and confident, and we cannot be moved. Our past is safe in His hands, our present is safe, and our future is safe. Then at the very end of this life, He will draw us safely into eternal joy. The life of the Christ-follower is a life of moving from glory to glory to glory. It does not mean that we will never have trouble, but it does mean that He will never leave us in trouble, and He will never stop being the light that guides us through darkness.

We are given a life that is a reflection of the life of Christ. This beautiful truth becomes food for our souls when we meditate on it. I am not referring to the Eastern meditation practice of focusing your mind on one particular thought, but rather the exercise of looking at a particular thought from many different perspectives to come to a deeper understanding. In our fast-paced modern lives, it is extremely hard to find time to explore the depths of God's Word. Back when I was in high school, I started the practice of scribbling down a Bible verse that I wanted think on more. I would tape it to my closet door at home or the inside of my locker at school. These days I almost always have a scrap of paper with a verse on it tucked into the pocket of my jeans. I have found this to be a powerful form of meditation. I read these verses throughout my week. I think about them as I drive to pick up my kids from school or wait in line at Starbucks. I start to see the truth of these verses from many different perspectives and contexts, and the Spirit shows me deeper and broader meanings. We know that David found quiet moments in the night to think on God's words. This is what he has done in Psalm 16. He affirms that the Lord has drawn lines in pleasant places. Then God directs his musings to show him how that truth has been manifested throughout his life. The glorious conclusion that he comes to is that the lines have always been and will always be drawn in pleasant places. He sees that his life will be redeemed by the life, death, and resurrection of Christ.

Meditate on Psalm 16. Jot it down on a post-it note, put it in your phone, or frame it in calligraphy. Say to yourself, "The lines have fallen for me in pleasant places." Reflect on how God has given you peace with your past, contentment in your present, and hope in your future.

GOD'S GOODNESS
PURSUES US

Surely goodness and mercy shall follow me
all the days of my life;
and I will dwell in the house of the LORD forever.
PSALM 23:6

PSALM 23 IS A RICH PSALM OF COMFORT.
It famously uses the analogy of God as our Shepherd,
leading us through valleys, giving us the rest and nourishment we need through life, protecting us from enemies, and even guiding us in death. I want to focus on
just one of the many comforts in this psalm. In verse six,
David says that goodness and mercy will follow him. In
his book, *The Lord is My Shepherd*, Robert Morgan offers
a helpful personification of goodness and mercy that
gives us a better understanding of what David means,

The Good Shepherd that goes before us has twin sheepdogs named "Goodness" and "Mercy" who follow us, nipping at our heels. "Goodness" scampers beside us with boundless energy, making sure we're surrounded with God's protective and proactive care. "Mercy" runs along behind, guarding our rear flanks, nipping at us if we lag, and retrieving us if we lose our way.*

The whole psalm is built on the shepherding metaphor. We are the sheep, unaware of impending enemies, yet easily scared by nonthreatening circumstances. Jesus is our Shepherd, our Guide, our Protector, and He has goodness and mercy as His helpers. He is leading, and they are following beside and behind to encourage us to stay on the right path.

What does this mean for us in our real lives? It means that as we raise our children or work at our jobs, God will give us many good gifts that we don't deserve to keep us focused in the right direction. Look for His mercies in your parenting. How often has He given you the grace you need to get through difficult milestones? Did you make it through childbirth? Through many sleepless nights? Through hundreds of Sundays with wiggling toddlers in the pew? He also showers His mercy by giving us joyful times. He gives us thousands of family

* Robert Morgan, *The Lord is My Shepherd: Resting in the Peace and Power of Psalm 23* (New York: Simon & Schuster, 2013), 164.

dinners, beautiful Christmases, school plays, new front teeth, learning to read, soccer games, family vacations, the awkwardness of pre-teen years, and the growing pains of watching our children become adults. All these gifts are showered on us even when we stumble. Look for His mercies in your career. Did He provide work for you when it was needed? Mark all the ways that He has guided you to take risks that paid off well, and mark all the ways that His provision found you when things did not pay off. Look for His mercies in your relationships. Has He provided friends who love you enough to rebuke you? Has He continually provided healing in your marriage? Are you marking all the good things—all the years of health and safety from disaster, the love of your spouse, the generosity of your parents? Can you start to see throughout it all that His sheepdogs have been nipping at your heels the whole time, giving grace and sweet memories and directing you from danger?

Goodness and mercy are certainly not only seen in parenting. They are with you in loneliness, in times of waiting, in illness, in grieving, in difficult marriages. They are always surrounding you, and you will see them if you look. Knowing this dispels our fears. Do you fear illness? Do you know that the Good Shepherd will send comfort and strength to you if you walk through illness? Do you fear loss? Do you know that He will be good even in loss, that He will provide the grace you need to walk through the painful milestones? Are you afraid He will not answer the prayers you have been lifting up for years? Look behind you. You will see that mercy and goodness have been with you through all the details of your waiting and you will find hope.

We don't always *feel* like things are good. We don't *feel* mercy flanking our backs. I know I have passed through many times in my life where I didn't feel like anything good was coming of it. This is the time to remember that we are like sheep. We don't really know what is going on. We are stupid. We need to follow the Shepherd and believe Him when He says not to be afraid. Look behind you for the tracks that goodness and mercy are leaving in the mud. When you see them behind you, you will believe that they will be with you in the future, and you will not be afraid.

Preach this truth to yourself in your prayers: "Surely good-ness and mercy will follow me all the days of my life." Saying this to yourself every day will open your eyes to all the ways that God is being good and merciful to you.

GOD CARES FOR
THE DYING

Precious in the sight of the LORD
Is the death of His saints.
PSALM 116:15

PSALM 116 IS A PRAISE TO GOD FOR deliverance from death. The writer talks about how he was brought low, greatly afflicted, and near to death. In the middle of his praise to the Lord for rescuing him, he says that the death of His saints is precious to God. This seems so strange because we do not think of death as precious. From our perspective, death is brutal, terrifying, and results in great loss for us. It is painful to watch someone die and it is painful to die. Timothy Keller, in his book *The Songs of Jesus*, translates the word "precious" as "costly."* The death of the saints is indeed very

* Keller, *The Songs of Jesus*, 299.

costly to God; it cost Him His own Son. Christ gave His
blood so that our death might be redeemed. In another
sense, the death of a saint is precious, meaningful, and
sweet to the Lord. When we die, we are safe with Christ,
God draws us to Himself, and He rejoices when another
saint enters into His presence.

In our culture, most of us do not have to face death
regularly. We will all lose loved ones and eventually lose
our own lives, but we are not confronted with mortality
on a daily basis. This is a blessing in many ways. We
have learned more about safety and health, and many of
us will be able to live long lives. Although death is not
frequently present, many of us live in fear of death. 2
Corinthians 5:1–6 gives us great comfort in this.

> For we know that if our earthly house, this tent, is
> destroyed, we have a building from God, a house
> not made with hands, eternal in the heavens. For
> in this we groan, earnestly desiring to be clothed
> with our habitation which is from heaven, if indeed,
> having been clothed, we shall not be found naked.
> For we who are in this tent groan, being burdened,
> not because we want to be unclothed, but further
> clothed, that mortality may be swallowed up by life.
> Now He who has prepared us for this very thing is
> God, who also has given us the Spirit as a guaran-
> tee. So we are always confident, knowing that while
> we are at home in the body we are absent from the
> Lord. For we walk by faith, not by sight. We are con-

fident, yes, well pleased rather to be absent from
the body and to be present with the Lord.

Our current bodies are temporary. Our current bodies are keeping us from full fellowship with Christ. When
we see loved ones die on this earth, Heaven is rejoicing
to welcome them. Their place in Heaven is fit perfectly
for them. C.S. Lewis explains it this way in *Problem of
Pain*: "Your place in heaven will seem to be made for you
and you alone, because you were made for it—made for
it stitch by stitch as a glove is made for a hand."* We
have nothing to fear on the other side of death. Jesus has
prepared a place for us, and He is anticipating the day
that we join Him.

We have nothing to fear about the process of our
death or the death of loved ones, either. It is hard to
watch loved ones suffer in pain as their bodies pass
away, and we miss them when they are gone from this
earth. But in the experience of death, God is there as a
help and a guide. In his book *The Lord is My Shepherd*,
Robert Morgan writes about Psalm 23:4 saying,

> Sometimes we would see a train coming that wasn't
> scheduled to stop at our station. It was an express
> train, and it whizzed by much faster, making the air
> rush past me like a windstorm. The platform would

---

* *The Problem of Pain*, 153.

tremble, and the roar would be unnerving. I'd be
hit by a shadow … yet I didn't suffer any injuries.*

He compares the shadow of the train to the shadow
of death. Christ was hit full force by the train, but now
we only experience the shadow of death. We do not
have to experience the entirety of the pain of real death.
The death of His faithful servants is precious to God. He
is there to oversee everything, He is near, He has already
emptied death of most of its pain, and He gently leads
His people safely to the other side.

*Have you lost loved ones? As you pray for comfort, preach this
truth from Psalm 116: "Precious in the sight of the* Lord *is the
death of His saints." Find comfort in knowing that God was
with them in their death.*

---

*   *The Lord is My Shepherd*, 118.

GOD CARES ABOUT
OUR HEART'S DESIRES

Trust in the LORD, and do good;
dwell in the land, and feed on His faithfulness.
Delight yourself also in the LORD,
and He shall give you the desires of your heart.

PSALM 37:3-4

THESE ARE SOME OF MY FAVORITE VERSES. The promise is bold and the path to the promise is sweet. David wrote this psalm as an old man. He exhorts his readers not to be afraid when they see the wicked prospering. He says that the righteous who patiently wait on God are going to be blessed and cared for. He has never seen the righteous forsaken, and God always exalts those who keep His ways.

It can be discouraging to see others around us prosper when we are not prospering, especially if those who are successful do not even love the Lord. Those of us who are in Christ have the power of the Spirit living in us. It seems as though we should be able to accomplish anything we set out to do. We see wicked parents abusing their children when we are praying to God for children of our own. Why are wicked parents given the blessing of children but we are not? We see men and women start successful businesses by manipulating and crushing others when we are working constantly to make ends meet. Why are the wicked prospering financially but we are not? Why are pastors who compromise the gospel seeing great growth in their churches? Why does it often look like the wicked are able to attain their heart's desires?

David gives us a comforting answer. He says to wait patiently on the Lord, to trust in Him, to do good, to dwell in the land, to feed on God's faithfulness, and to delight in Him. If we do these things, we have a promise awaiting us: He shall give us the desires of our hearts. David tells us how we are supposed to live so that we will see God's blessing on us.

Remind yourself of these six things:

First, we have to rest in God's timing. This is what it means to wait patiently for Him. We are not in a hurry to achieve our goals and dreams. We are not grasping.

Second, we trust Him to do good to us. We believe that He is kind, wise, and has our best interest in His plan. We trust that He will not give us a stone when we ask for bread.

Third, we are to do good. We are to look for ways to serve, to give, to bless others. We are to obey the commands of God found in Scripture.

Fourth, David says to dwell in the land (v. 3). For the Israelites this would have meant to literally stay in the promised land. For us this means to plant ourselves wherever God has put us. We should be faithful to do whatever work we have been given that is right in front of us. We are to cultivate community and plant the gospel where we are.

Fifth, we are to feed on His faithfulness. We are to literally nourish our souls by remembering all the faithful acts He has shown us. This is how we preach to ourselves. We are to study the stories in Scripture and remind ourselves constantly of His deliverance, His kindness, and His mercy. This becomes our food and nourishment for our soul.

Last, we are to delight in Him. We are to find joy in knowing Him more fully. We are to worship Him. We are to sing to Him. We are to speak to Him, listen to Him, and enjoy our relationship with Him.

David reassures us that when we live this way, God will bring our desires to fulfillment. He helps us turn our focus away from our hopes and onto God. He shows us what a life of patiently resting in God looks like. As we delight in knowing and serving God, our own desires align with God's will. When we submit ourselves to accepting whatever story God has for us, our desires turn from seeking to change our story to desiring to bring

His glory about in our stories. When I was eight weeks pregnant with my son, my doctor took one look at the ultrasound and told me he would not live. His body was healthy, but mine was not. I waited for a miscarriage but it did not come. Every four weeks I went back for a check-up and my doctor was surprised to hear a beating heart every time. Unlike David in Psalm 37, I did not have wicked men prospering around me, but I did have a strong desire in my heart. I prayed many times for my baby to live, but I knew I had to wait for an answer. Sometimes pregnancy can seem so long. I turned to Psalm 37 to train me how I should live while I waited on God. I learned more about how to rest in trust, how to delight in and feed on His faithfulness, and how to dwell where He had put me. He did not fail in His promise. My son was born healthy and fat two weeks before his due date.

Is there something you desire? Do you have deep hopes that you have yet to see God fulfill? Learn from David how to live while you wait on God. Preach this truth to yourself: "Delight yourself also in the LORD, and He shall give you the desires of your heart."

GOD AS A ROCK

My soul, wait silently for God alone,
for my expectation is from Him.
He only is my rock and my salvation;
He is my defense; I shall not be moved.
In God is my salvation and my glory;
the rock of my strength, and my refuge, is in God.
Trust in Him at all times, you people;
pour out your heart before Him;
God is a refuge for us. *Selah*
PSALM 62:5–8

WHEN WE ARE WAITING ON THE LORD TO answer a prayer, we have to feed our souls with encouragement from Scripture. We need to surround ourselves with encouraging, godly people. We need to continue in prayer. David says in Psalm 62 that he is able to wait silently for God. He has found peace and contentment in the waiting. We see other places in the Psalms that

David is pleading with God to "hurry up," but this psalm is more patient. He reveals his secret to finding this patience in verse eight where he commands us to pour our hearts out before God. This is what David has done, and it was by doing this that he found the peace and strength he needed to wait on God's timing and deliverance.

When we are waiting for God, it is easy to feel impatient, to wonder how long, to frantically search for immediate solutions, to discuss our problem with anyone who will listen. This is not the way to find peace. The way to find peace is to pour out our hearts to God. We need to tell Him how much it hurts, how long it has been, how we are afraid of the outcome. This is the only way we will be able to ride out storms. When we are praying for a spouse and each year our age makes us feel more desperate to find someone, we need to pour that out to God. When we are praying for a better job, and each month gets us more behind financially, we need to pour that out to God. When we are pregnant again with a surprise baby, and each nauseous day makes us more afraid that we won't be able to handle another one, we need to pour that out to God.

I have struggled long with chronic headaches. I saw a doctor who sent me to a chiropractor. The chiropractor said I was allergic to wheat, so I went to an allergist. The allergist put me on supplements and a very restrictive diet that made no difference in my pain. The chiropractor told me to exercise more; the naturopath told me to stop exercising. I had a headache either way. The

primary care doctor gave me a prescription for pain re-
lievers that did nothing. After more than a year of dead-
end rabbit trails, I just stopped. I canceled all my doctor
appointments and threw away my supplements. For
months I had been desperately chasing after solutions.
The whole time I had been praying for healing and for
perseverance, but I had not been completely letting my
strength and hope come from God. I had been letting
my hope rest in finding a solution with one of the many
doctors I saw. I had not been patient. Psalm 62 came to
me as a message of hope. My peace does not come from
finding the right solution; my peace comes from telling
God about my hardship and patiently waiting for Him
to either guide me to healing or to give me the strength
to live with pain. Have you been crying out to God for
help in your life? Are you resting in the hope that He
hears you and that He will provide a clear path? When
you strive for a resolution, be sure that all your hope of
solution is placed firmly in the power of God and not in
your own abilities.

When David pours his heart out to God, he finds unwavering hope. He describes it as standing on a rock;
God is his rock. When David stands on Him, he cannot be moved. He is strong. His peace does not waver.
He is not desperate for a solution. He is content to wait
out the trial as long as God has planned. He does not
have to share all the details of his pain with everyone he
meets. He is raw before God, and God grants him protection from worry and fear and anxiety and desperation.

Waiting on God does not mean we pretend like nothing is wrong. Waiting on Him means that we look to Him to give us the protection we need to withstand the waiting. He always comes to be our refuge.

Are you facing a challenge in your life? Pour out your heart to God. Tell Him all the details. Preach this truth to yourself as a reminder that He will bring you patience in your struggle: "My soul, wait silently for God alone, for my expectation is from Him. He only is my rock and my salvation; He is my defense; I shall not be moved."

GOD AS THE SOURCE
OF LONGSUFFERING

But You, O Lord, are a God
full of compassion, and gracious,
Longsuffering and abundant in mercy and truth.

PSALM 86:15

PSALM 86 IS ANOTHER PSALM WRITTEN BY David. He is in trouble, and he is begging God to help him. He shows his strong assurance in God's complete forgiveness. He even calls himself holy because he believes with all his heart that God has covered him in righteousness. He calls upon God's character in verse fifteen as a reason why God should deliver him. He says that God is compassionate, gracious, longsuffering, and abundant in mercy and truth.

God is incredibly patient with His people. When His people were complaining about living in Egypt,

He orchestrated a grand plan for deliverance. When He brought them out to the wilderness, they were consumed with fear. Again He swooped in and delivered them at the last minute. When they complained about their hunger and their thirst, He provided for them. He cared for them for years while they whined at Him. He asked for their trust, and they made a golden calf. But God continued to pour out mercy on His people.

2 Peter 3:8–9 says, "But, beloved, do not forget this one thing, that with the Lord one day is as a thousand years, and a thousand years as one day. The Lord is not slack concerning His promise, as some count slackness, but is longsuffering toward us, not willing that any should perish but that all should come to repentance." God is not fast to act by our standards. He acts in His own time because He does not wish for any to fall away. God is longsuffering. He suffers for a long time for our sakes. He is patient with us, allowing us to make many mistakes, forgiving us for them all, guiding us gently and slowly towards holiness.

Longsuffering is one of the fruits of the Spirit found in Galatians 5. It is one of the virtues that the Spirit works in our hearts as we worship and follow Christ. We need to be longsuffering with each other. When someone sins against us, we need to be ready to forgive and show them kindness. When they sin against us again, we need to suffer long for them, forgiving them again. When someone inconveniences us or annoys us, we need to be ready to overlook the offense. This is required most frequently with family members. When we live alongside others we will have the opportunity for many offenses. Small children wake up too early too many days in a row, parents try to control us, in-laws offer unwanted opinions, siblings are given the unique gift of knowing exactly how to annoy us. In families we are given countless small opportunities to imitate God in His longsuffering. David tells us that God is full of compassion and mercy for us. He remembers that God has extended great mercy and patience to him. His meditation on this characteristic of God gives him the strength to suffer patiently at the hand of his own father-in-law, King Saul.

Patience and longsuffering are not only needed in relationships. They are also needed in trials that we face. God often allows trials to continue for a long time in order to work this virtue in our hearts. We cannot be long-suffering unless we have suffered long. We are often in a rush to get to the other side of a trial. We are desperate for things to resolve. We can find contentment and rest right in the midst of suffering when we remember that God is using this to create the fruit of the Spirit in our hearts. Do not be discouraged if your trial seems to be dragging on for a long time. God hears you. He promises to hear us and He promises to deliver us.

In our family, we love to celebrate Advent during the four weeks leading up to Christmas. I spend some time right after Thanksgiving selecting and wrapping little books, games, toys, and chocolates. We write numbers on the packages and attach a verse that tells part of the story of Christmas. Every day of Advent the children get to open one of these presents. Part of my reason for instituting this tradition is because it is so much fun, but I also want to teach my children something about waiting and patience. Advent is the season of waiting, but it has a joyful anticipation connected to it. Whenever we wait on God for anything, there is a joyful anticipation at the end. He does not allow any suffering or waiting unless He plans to bring about glory from it. We always have that to hope in. Even during the seasons of waiting, God gives us many small, delightful gifts. He gives us friends and good food and wine and books to bring joy to our hearts even while we walk through trials that seem endless. God doesn't train us in longsuffering without also leaving lots of little gifts along the way.

Are you struggling to be patient with someone in your life? Are you struggling to be patient with a situation in your life? Ask God to give you patience and longsuffering. In your prayer, include these words of David: "You, O Lord, are a God full of compassion, and gracious, longsuffering and abundant in mercy and truth." Remind yourself that you are praying to the One who has been patient with you, who is longsuffering, and who will strengthen you to suffer in patience.

GOD'S PROTECTION
IN FEAR

You have hedged me behind and before,
and laid Your hand upon me.
Such knowledge is too wonderful for me;
it is high, I cannot attain it.

PSALM 139:5–6

Psalm 139 is written by David and describes God's perfect knowledge of His servants. David describes about how God searches his heart and sees his actions (verses 23–24). He knows the inward and the outward. David acknowledges that there is no place we can go without God being there, and there is no thought we can think without God seeing it (verses 7–12). Even in the darkest places of our thoughts, God is there, ready and willing to shed His light. David relates how God formed him before he was born and laid out all his days for him. "Your eyes saw my substance, being yet unformed. And in Your book they all were written, the days fashioned for me, when as yet there were none of them" (verse 16). For the disobedient, it is terrifying that God knows and sees everything about them. For the righteous, there is great comfort here. We cannot go through any painful valley without God. He is in the depths, and He is on the heights. We cannot escape His love or His care.

When my husband and I had been married three months, we traveled to Oregon to visit his parents and help with cattle branding. I was making lunch in the house when I saw two friends dragging my husband up the muddy hill. He had been kicked in the face by a large calf and was slipping in and out of consciousness. We were too far from the hospital to wait for an ambulance, so my father-in-law raced us across the dirt roads while I sat in the back of the truck and tried to keep my husband awake. He was incoherent and would barely open his eyes. His face and shirt were covered in blood and mud. I needed Psalm 139 that day. The words, "You have hedged me behind and before, and laid Your hand upon me" replayed through my mind, and I found great comfort in knowing that God's hands were surrounding us. Nothing could penetrate God's protecting hedges unless He allowed it. My husband escaped brain damage. The calf's hoof barely missed his eye, and he was released with some butterfly bandages and a minor concussion.

God has built a wall around us, and His own hand is covering us. Nothing can breach the wall. We are safe even when we don't feel safe. David goes on to say that even if he made his bed in Sheol, God would be there. "Indeed, the darkness shall not hide from You, but the night shines as the day; the darkness and the light are both alike to You" (verse 12). The darkest places are not dark to God, because He is light. His light overpowers the darkness.

There are many dark times that we will face in this world: difficult illnesses, torn relationships, deaths, infertility, and poverty. There are also less dramatic events that cause us to be afraid: a child who needs surgery, a husband who becomes increasingly distant, a teenager who is making unwise choices, icy roads, credit card debt, tax audits, undiagnosed sickness, and the list goes on. Each of us can easily find an area where we are tempted to fear the world instead of trusting God. This is when we need Psalm 139 to be written on our hearts. When you are tempted to fear, use Psalm 139 as a script to give gratitude to God. Thank Him that He sees your sitting down and your rising up. Thank Him that He has hedged you in with His wall of protection. Thank Him that there is no darkness where His light does not shine. Thank Him that He formed you and made a plan for each of your days on earth. Thanking Him is offering praise to Him, and offering praise reminds us of all He has done for us. Remembering His goodness casts out fear. Gratitude is praise, and praise is remembering, and remembering is courage.

When your fears arise, preach to your own heart the truth of God's protection from Psalm 139: "You have hedged me behind and before, and laid Your hand upon me."

GOD'S GIFT OF COURAGE

Be merciful to me, O God, for man would swallow me up;
fighting all day he oppresses me.
My enemies would hound me all day,
for there are many who fight against me, O Most High.
Whenever I am afraid, I will trust in You.
In God (I will praise His word),
In God I have put my trust;
I will not fear.
What can flesh do to me?

PSALM 56:1–4

FEAR IS ONE OF THE MOST CRIPPLING emotions. It controls many of our decisions, actions, and reactions. This is not the way it should be. Ever since the Fall, God has been telling His people not to be afraid. Psalm 56 is written by David when he was in a real crisis with the Philistines. He fled from Saul to Achish the

King of Gath, but David did not find the welcome he was hoping for, and he had to act insane to protect his own life. He had a real reason to be afraid in his situation, but he found courage in turning to God for help.

Trusting in God is believing that He cares about our situation. In verse 8, David writes, "You number my wanderings; put my tears into Your bottle; are they not in Your book?" The comfort of knowing that God is paying attention to his suffering and keeping track of all the pain brings David courage. He knows he can trust in a God who is attentive.

Sometimes we face situations where we must have active courage like David needed at Gath. We must be courageous during situations like interviewing for a job, giving birth to a child, moving to a new city, facing debilitating illness, and many other moments that might make us nervous or fearful. God is there to give us strength and courage in those situations. This is the kind of courage that David needed when he protected his sheep from lions, when he killed Goliath, and when he was fleeing from Saul. When my husband was around eight years old, he lived deep in the woods of Eastern Oregon. One afternoon while he was exploring the family property, a cougar jumped out of a tree and landed face-to-face with him. He tells our children that he froze and looked the cougar straight in the eyes until it ran away. God was with him in that moment to give him the courage he needed to be brave.

Another kind of courage we need more regularly is passive courage—courage to *not* do things. We need courage to deny our desires, courage to not insist on our own plans instead of submitting to God's, courage not to defend ourselves when we believe we are right, courage to not go after our own pursuits when our families need us. We need courage to control our words around a critical mother-in-law or an annoying child. We need courage to obey our parents even when we disagree with them. We need courage to give up what we want for the sake of someone else, believing that God will raise us up. Passive courage takes the risk that we will be overlooked, criticized, misjudged, mistreated.

Charles Spurgeon famously said in one of his sermons, "Have you consciously thought of God standing with you?"* This is a powerful mental practice. When we think of God actually standing by our side, we can find the strength to have courage in challenging circumstances. If we think of God standing with us when we are criticized unjustly, we can find the courage to be quiet. We know He sees that we are righteous. If we think of God standing with us when we want to be selfish, we can find the courage to serve someone else. We know that He sees our sacrifice and He will bless us for it.

Courage is needed in all of life, because fear is a lifelong temptation for many of us. Fear brings with it all sorts of sin. Disrespect is fueled by the fear of being

---

* C.H. Spurgeon, "Jacob's Waking Explanation." Modified by Robert J. Morgan, *The Lord is My Shepherd*, 126.

controlled by someone in authority over us. Envy is fueled by the fear that someone else is better than we are. Sexual sin can be fueled by the fear that God isn't going to give us a righteous context for sex. Worry is fueled by the fear that God won't give us grace in the future. Courage is the antithesis of fear and courage protects us from all the sins that fear drives us towards. It is a result of trust and praise, rather than worry and anxiety. We can be facing extremely terrifying situations that can potentially cause us real and lasting hurt, but even in the most dire circumstances we do not have to give way to fear.

Are you afraid of an upcoming event in your life? Are you afraid of making a sacrifice because you fear never having want you want? When you ask the Lord for courage, affirm this truth to yourself: "Whenever I am afraid, I will trust in You. In God I have put my trust. I will not fear. What can man do to me?"

GOD'S GIFT OF PEACE

The LORD will give strength to His people;
the LORD will bless His people with peace.
PSALM 29:11

GOD PROMISES STRENGTH AND PEACE. This is often hard for us to believe because we live in a world that is not yet peaceful. There are real wars and terrorist attacks, but there are many other things that steal our internal peace. In our culture, we are more commonly dealing with wars in our hearts. Worry, anxiety, fear, discontent, and restlessness are the worst enemies of peace. We live in a stressed-out culture, and stress takes away our strength. Strength and peace go hand in hand. To solve this cultural problem there is no end to stress-relieving solutions. My doctor told me that it is estimated about one-third of the population of the US is on anti-depressants, and that anti-depressants are the most commonly prescribed medication. Even in the natural medicine culture, millions of dollars are being spent on essential oils which claim to give you peace and joy. Others turn to meditation and yoga to clear their heads and find peace. Man is hungry for peace on his own terms.

While I do believe that there may be a time for using things like essential oils or yoga or even prescription anti-depressants, we must view these things as gifts and tools, and certainly not place our trust in them. God is the source of all peace and of all strength. Augustine of Hippo said it this way: "You arouse us so that praising you may bring us joy, because you have made us and drawn us to yourself, and our heart is unquiet until it rests in you."*

We cannot find real peace if we are searching for it in a DoTerra bottle. Our worries and our fears will not cease unless we have offered them to God. We are made for God, to glorify and enjoy Him. Philippians 4:6-7 tells us it is by drawing near to God in gratitude that we find the peace to guard our hearts and minds. Our hearts will not find peace unless they are resting in God, resting in the belief that He is writing our stories perfectly, resting in the saturation of His love. We can try to take a sleeping pill when our anxiety keeps us awake at night, and while it may help us get some sleep, it will not give us peace and strength. We have to confess our anxieties. We have to let them die. We have to give them over to

* Augustine of Hippo, *The Confessions*, trans. Maria Boulding, OSB (Hyde Park, NY: New City Press, 1997), Book 1.1.

God. We have to let Him control all the aspects of our lives that are keeping us awake.

When I was in college, I realized that my life was not going in the direction I had been hoping for. I was anxious about it, and it constantly gnawed away at my peace. I had to learn to daily let go of what I wanted. I learned that when my mind began to wander to wishing for the plans that I had hoped for, I had to immediately pray and offer my plans up to God. I had to remind myself that He was in control and ask Him to take charge of the situation. I had to continually run to Him and find my strength in Him. To be perfectly honest, that is a process that has never changed, although the content of my temptation to worry has changed. The change in context doesn't erase the battle. I still have to give Him my worries, fears, anxieties, hopes, and disappointments daily. I have to sacrifice them as a priest sacrificed animals to the Lord: kill them and let them go up in smoke to God. I have no peace unless I have laid out my concerns to Him and turned my back on my own fears.

Giving our anxiety and stress to God is only helpful if we understand who He is. He is the One who loves us. He is the One who is caring for us and who can't forget us. Isaiah 49:15–16 says, "Can a woman forget her nursing child, and not have compassion on the son of her womb? Surely they may forget, yet I will not forget you. See, I have inscribed you on the palms of My hands."

When we are confident that God loves us even more than a mother loves her newborn child, then we can confidently give our worries and fears to Him, knowing that He can't forget us. Remembering us is part of who He is. Peace is what He promises to us when we run to Him, and peace is what gives us strength. We don't have to live in stress like the rest of the world. Our hearts can find rest when they find rest in God. Believe Him when He says that He will bless you with peace.

Examine your heart and find what is stealing your peace. Offer your hardship to the Lord and speak this truth to yourself: "The LORD will give strength to His people; the LORD will bless His people with peace."

GOD OVERCOMES ANXIETY

In the multitude of my anxieties within me,
Your comforts delight my soul.
PSALM 94:19

PSALM 94 IS A PRAYER TO GOD TO JUDGE
evil in the world. The writer sees wickedness triumphing
in the world, and pleads with God to come to the cause
of the righteous. He then moves to assurance of God's
mercy, and assurance that God hears his cries. In verse
19, he acknowledges that his only comfort in anxiety is
the Lord. In the previous chapter we saw how God promises to give peace to those who seek Him. In this passage
we can continue to see how we can let go of anxiety.

The troubling thing about the sin of anxiety is that
when it takes root, it feeds on itself and is harder to kill,
but it is extremely important that Christians gain victory

173

over anxiety. It is a terrible state of mind that causes us to doubt the goodness of the Lord on all fronts, it steals our gratitude and our joy, and it even changes our bodies, physically causing all sorts of symptoms that doctors blame on "stress." When we learn from the psalmists, we find that God's comforts are the medicine we need to make our souls rejoice again.

God's comforts are all over Scripture. They are His promises to love, protect, hear, and bless us. We have to train our minds to focus on the comforts instead of the anxieties. We must learn to change our well-worn thought patterns and carve out new ways of thinking. We have to be diligent in controlling what thoughts we entertain in our minds.

Ed Welch wrote an excellent little book on anxiety called *When I Am Afraid.** In his book, he recommends laying out all your worries and anxieties, and then standing them up against the promises of God. You will find that you would make a terrible prophet. You worry about your husband driving home from a work trip in a blizzard, which is like prophesying to yourself that God will not protect him. We need to remember that we are not prophets. God is the One who is in control and determines the future. This is truth, this is one of God's comforts, and this is what we should let our minds rest on. Just as the writer of Psalm 94 became anxious because of the evil in the world, we become

* Edward T. Welch, *When I Am Afraid: A Step-by-Step Guide Away from Fear and Anxiety* (Greensboro, NC: New Growth, 2008).

anxious when we believe the lie that the painful effects of sin and evil will be triumphant.

Dr. Welch also draws attention to the story of the Israelites in the wilderness after fleeing Egypt, when they were fraught with anxiety. They were afraid of not having the quality of food that they had in Egypt. In response to their requests, God sent manna, a substance that contained every necessary ingredient for health. He gave them exactly what they needed to get through that day. He told them not to gather anything for the next day, and they had to trust that He would send exactly what they needed for each day on that day. Dr. Welch compares manna to God's grace. God gives the grace we need for each day, but He does not give us today the grace we need for tomorrow. Tomorrow He will give the grace for tomorrow.

Looking for God's comforts often means we have to look behind us. We have to remember how He gave us manna yesterday when we needed it and believe that He will give us manna tomorrow. If we are anxious about money, we should remember all the times He has provided for us. When we train our minds to focus on those things, we have faith to face the future without worry. If we are worried about our health, we should remember all the times He gave us grace to get through each medical procedure and how many illnesses He has healed. We have to train our minds to focus on His provision in the past, instead of letting our thoughts run wild with possibilities of how He might not provide in the future.

God's faithfulness in the past is the comfort that He offers to soothe our fears. This is why Scripture is full of so many stories. We are to remember the stories, even the ones that happened thousands of years ago. God does not change. If He is powerful enough to shut the mouths of lions, He is powerful enough to help you with your tomorrow. Fill your mind with these stories when fear and anxiety try to take hold. Let these comforts delight your soul.

When you are overtaken with anxiety and fear, remind yourself of this truth: "In the multitude of my anxieties within me, Your comforts delight my soul." List some of the ways that God has sent His comforts to you and triumphed over evils in your life. The memory of His grace will be your strength.

GOD AS THE DELIVERER
FROM ENEMIES

I will wait for You, O You his Strength;
for God is my defense.
My God of mercy shall come to meet me;
God shall let me see my desire on my enemies.

PSALM 59:9–10

DAVID WROTE PSALM 59 WHEN HE FOUND
out that Saul had sent a group of men to kill him in his
own house. The psalm is about how his enemies are rising up against him, seeking to take his life, even though
he has not sinned. He states in verses 3–4 that it is not
his fault that they are seeking to attack him. Instead of
immediately taking matters into his own hands, he turns
to God for help and deliverance. He decides to wait, believing that God will come to meet him with mercy.

This psalm is a great comfort if we are ever in a situation where we are being slandered or mistreated. We can find comfort in knowing that God is just and merciful and He is a defense for the righteous. Defense can mean an actual physical barrier to keep enemies from attacking, but it also can mean someone who defends us like an attorney in a court of law. A defense can argue for righteousness and can protect us from charges brought against us. We may face many personal enemies in our lives who seek to destroy us by spreading lies, attack our work or our character, speak unkindly to us, hurt us physically and emotionally, or steal from us. Many times the most painful wounds are those made by people closest to us: friends, parents, spouses, or even our children. David knew hurt from all of these, and he called upon God to defend him.

Although our enemies are often people, it is more common that we will be daily bombarded with enemies that are in our hearts. We face a myriad of temptations regularly that seek to attack our faithfulness to God. Personal relationships are often the spark that creates the temptation. When we are tempted to speak unkindly to our children or to criticize our husbands, this is an enemy that is seeking to destroy our family. When we are tempted to be discontent and envious, this is an enemy seeking to steal our joy. We may be tempted to make idols out of many things in our lives: money, organization, fitness, fashion, food, or technology. The temptation to love things more than our Lord is a huge enemy.

Few of us will have men sent from our father-in-law to attack us in our homes like David. Our enemies are more subtle, and the first step to defeating them is to identify them. I began a simple practice recently that I have found extremely helpful in identifying the enemies in my own life. Look at any area of your life that you are struggling with: marriage, finances, parenthood, relationships, time management, etc. Ask God to show you areas of your walk that are in danger. Ask Him to show you where you have made idols. Ask Him to show you the enemies. Maybe you are struggling in your marriage because your husband is lazy and you have a hard time treating him with respect. The enemy you need to fight is disrespect, not his laziness. Maybe you yell at your children because they are loud and don't obey quickly. Your enemy in your parenting is your lack of self-control, not their childish lifestyle. Maybe you struggle with your parents because they make ridiculously restrictive rules. The enemy you need to fight is disrespect, not their choice in rules. Maybe your enemy is an area of life that you consider yourself to be doing really well in. Maybe you are a financial wizard. Ask God to show you if you have made money your idol, to show you if you have loved money more than His people. Your pride in your finances could be an enemy. Ask Him to show you if you have made an idol out of other areas like your work or your good grades or your athletic abilities.

Once you have identified your temptations, you can start to see them as the enemies that they are. When we give in to these temptations, they destroy us. We need to cultivate a desire to destroy these enemies. Instead of giving in to the temptation to yell at your children, wait on God. He is your defense. He will destroy the anger and frustration and set you free from this enemy. Identifying our enemies is the first step to praying for their destruction.

If there is one thing we must learn from the Psalms, it is that God loves to deliver. He loves to destroy our enemies. He loves to bring people down who have hurt His faithful people. He loves to destroy any area of our lives that will hurt us. Whenever you are struggling, look at all the idols that God is breaking down within you. Look at all the ways that He is destroying your enemies. The God of mercy is coming to meet you.

When you are struggling to gain victory over a specific sin which is an enemy against your soul, do not look to your own strength. Confess your sin to the Lord and preach this truth to yourself, "God shall let me see my desire on my enemies."

GOD IN CONTROL

God is our refuge and strength,
a very present help in trouble.
Therefore we will not fear,
even though the earth be removed,
and though the mountains be carried
into the midst of the sea;
though its waters roar and be troubled,
though the mountains shake with its swelling. *Selah*

PSALM 46:1–3

GOD IS OUR REFUGE. THE FIRST THREE verses of Psalm 46 say that we have nothing to fear even if the earth implodes. He will still be our help. Even if wars erupt, He is the One who breaks weapons. The worst disasters can befall the world, and He will help us. The psalm says that He is a "very present" help; He is not distant when trouble comes. He is present and near.

It is difficult to fully grasp the omnipotence of God because our abilities are so far below His power. In Mark 4, the disciples are fearful because a storm is raging on the sea as they are trying to sail across. When they wake Jesus, He simply stands on the deck of the boat and tells the wind and the waves to calm down, and they do. If Jesus is able to command something so uncontrollable as the wind and the sea, what else do you think He can command? He is powerful enough to command cancer, telling it when to cease and when to take life. He is powerful enough to control money, deciding who will have it and who will not. He is powerful enough to control fertility, deciding at what time conception will occur. This is where Psalm 46 is such a comfort. The psalm is declaring that God is commanding over all the earth, no matter what happens. When we believe that we serve an all-powerful God, we are safe to relinquish control over all the details of our lives.

It is important for us to regularly affirm that we believe God is in complete control because this produces the fruit of peace and patience, and (as the psalm says) this belief dispels fear. When we believe that God is in control, we are able to willingly submit to all authorities He places over us. If our boss is asking an unreasonable amount of work in exchange for an unreasonably low wage, we can find peace because we know that God has power over our boss. When we believe God is in control, we can trust Him with our children. It is easy for parents to put their belief in restrictive rules, thinking that a good environment will produce a good child. God has power over our children. Our efforts to control everything in their lives has no power.

When we believe God is in control, we can face illness with deep hope. The world tells us to trust in restrictive diets, essential oils, medication, and surgical intervention. But these things have no power apart from God. When we believe God is in control, we feel safe during financial hardship. He has the power to direct money wherever He pleases. When Jesus was short on tax money He told Peter to go fishing. Peter found enough money in the mouth of the fish to pay for taxes (Matthew 17). Our budgeting systems hold no power.

In Matthew 8 a centurion comes to Jesus begging for healing for his sick servant. Jesus offers to come to the man's house, but he refuses. He asks Jesus just to speak the word of the healing. He is a man in authority and he sees his orders result in action. He acknowledges that he believes Jesus has authority and power over healing. He knows that Jesus' words will result in action. Jesus says this man has the greatest faith he has seen in all of Israel. Jesus equates an acknowledgement of His power with a confession of faith. When we acknowledge God's power over every area of our life, we are living a life of faith.

Ask the Lord to show you areas of your life where you are seeking to have control and power. Remind yourself that you

are safe to let go of those things because God is in control over everything on the earth by affirming these words: "God is our refuge and strength, a very present help in trouble. Therefore we will not fear, even though the earth be removed."

GOD AS OUR TEACHER

As for God, His way is perfect;
The word of the LORD is proven;
He is a shield to all who trust in Him.
For who is God, except the LORD?
And who is a rock, except our God?
It is God who arms me with strength,
and makes my way perfect.
He makes my feet like the feet of deer,
And sets me on my high places.
He teaches my hands to make war,
so that my arms can bend a bow of bronze.
You have also given me the shield of Your salvation;
Your right hand has held me up,
Your gentleness has made me great.
You enlarged my path under me,
so my feet did not slip.

PSALM 18:30–36

GOD IS OUR GUIDE. WHEN LIFE IS GOOD, when life is hard, when life is boring, God is always leading us and teaching us and providing for us. I have found it to be particularly easy to acknowledge God's leadership when we are in stressful times. When my husband and I were driving across the country, moving two thousand miles with our two tiny children in the back seat, it was easy for me to keep my eyes peeled for how God was going to strengthen us. But when life is fairly normal and we are just racing along through school pickups and packing lunches and changing diapers and trying to figure out the best way to organize the Legos, I can easily forget that God is holding me up with His right hand.

In Psalm 18, David is praising God for delivering him from Saul again. God had to guide David in many details of his life in order to help him escape Saul's exhausting pursuit. When David looked back over the events, he saw how God had guided him, given him strength, protected him, taught him to fight, upheld him, and made him great. God laid out a path for him, and David can see that he was delivered from Saul because of God's guidance, not by his own strength.

As I am in the middle of raising small children, I want to learn to imitate God in how I parent them. One of the things we see here is that God is a patient guide. He equips David with what he needs to face his challenge, he teaches him skills, and he gives him a path. God is not always very obvious in His guidance. It frequently feels like we are supposed to figure things out for ourselves. But when we look back, we can see that He has been guiding us the whole way. In the same way, I hope to be a guide to my children, not in the sense that I am always telling them exactly what to do forever. To imitate God in guiding children, I need to create a life for them that is intentionally steering them in a certain direction, and I need to equip them with the skills they need to go that way.

This is very simple in the young years (where we are). Every few months I make a list of things that I can see each of my children needs to work on. The two-year-old needs to learn self-control and needs to be potty trained, the four-year-old needs to learn to write her letters and needs to come more quickly when I call, the six-year-old needs more physical activity and needs to learn to fold her laundry. Then I plan out our days so that we are working on these things one small piece at a time. I am setting a pathway for them, and each day giving them small pieces of information or discipline or activities that will train them to walk down the pathway they need to go. I want to give them the abilities they need in order to successfully sit through church or write words or play a sport or clean their room.

God is exhaustively intentional with how He directs our stories. As I seek to reflect this in parenting, I also want to recognize God's intentional guidance and training in my own life. My own pathway is being laid out by God and He is daily equipping me in very small doses to meet the goal that He has set for me. God trains us gently and patiently with small trials in order to give us greater faith. The strength that He arms us with makes our way perfect. Through His patient guidance, He makes us strong enough to do things we never thought we could. When we are called to do something that is hard, or something that we do not want to do, this psalm gives us hope that God will teach us along the way.

Consider the path your life is taking. Reflect on the truth that God has laid out that pathway for you. Reflect on the truth that He is teaching you the skills you need to accomplish each goal He has set before you.

GOD AS THE GUIDE OF OUR DECISIONS

The LORD shall preserve you from all evil;
He shall preserve your soul.
The LORD shall preserve your going out and your coming in
from this time forth, and even forevermore.
PSALM 121:7–8

REGRET IS THE PIOUS COUSIN OF UNBELIEF. When we look back over the story of our life and we agonize over moments that we wish we had done differently, we are essentially disbelieving that God was guiding us, and we are "piously" trying to take the blame. If we look at our story and we see sin, we should confess our sin. However, we must then believe that it is forgiven and forgotten. We must move on because that is what God does. We are not permitted to dwell on a sin or a mistake that God does not dwell on. Even David, when he regretted his actions of adultery and murder, confessed his sins, and found full assurance of God's forgiveness. When we dwell on our past mistakes, we are proclaiming that our feelings about the past are more important than God's words of forgiveness. We are not to spend our lives wishing we had done something differently. Even if we sinned in the past, God has already used that evil to bring about good in our story. He will continue to use even our darkest moments to bring light, because that is what He always does. Regret about the past can make us fearful to make decisions in the present. Psalm 121 is a song of hope. It says that God is our help, our Keeper who never sleeps, our shade, our preserver. He will watch over all our steps in the future, and He has watched over all our steps in the past.

My first baby was delivered by emergency cesarean section after a sudden placenta abruption. There was no option of labor. We had to save her life, and by God's kindness in giving us a skilled doctor, she was delivered healthy and alert. As more children came along, there was always the question of continuing to deliver by C-section or not. A variety of circumstances led us to choosing C-sections. I have no regrets in our choice. I'm thankful that we have had three C-sections and three babies, even though I know that in some ways this is the harder road. It is most definitely the more expensive road. It has definitely brought more criticism from other women. But God guided us then as we made those decisions. He wanted us in those hospitals with those doctors and nurses and anesthe-siologists. He wanted His light, which shines in us, to be present there with those people for some reason. I may not always see the reason why He has guided us to one thing and away from another, but I know that the reasons are always much bigger than our own list of pros and cons. Believing that He was and is guiding us squelches out room for regret. Whenever I find myself questioning decisions I have made, I speak Psalm 121 to my own heart. I am reminded that God promises to preserve all my steps. There was not a moment when He left me alone.

When you look over your story, you have the option of highlighting what you want. You can look over your story and see all the trials, believing that your life has just been one struggle to the next. You can look over your story and wish you had done everything different-ly. You can retell how your story would have worked out if you had chosen differently. But this is not wise, and you are not believing God when He says that He preserves all your steps. Even if your past actions were sinful, it is unbelief to dwell on the regret. God has forgiven and forgotten. Try retelling your story high-lighting His goodness. When you start to see the past through the belief that God has always guided you, you will find that His mercy is an engulfing wave and you will wonder how you ever doubted that He was guiding you the whole time. You will see His mercy is far more frequent than His correction, and even His correction is a mercy. You will see that He guided you carefully through every decision. You will see that He preserved every step that you took, which will make you bold so that you can make decisions about the future.

*Do you have regrets in your life? Do you have big decisions to make? As you pray for peace and guidance, remind yourself of this truth from Psalm 121: "The L*ORD* shall preserve your going out and your coming in from this time forth, and even forevermore."*

GOD AS THE GIVER
OF PROSPERITY

Unless the LORD builds the house,
they labor in vain who build it;
unless the LORD guards the city,
the watchman stays awake in vain.
It is vain for you to rise up early,
to sit up late,
to eat the bread of sorrows;
for so He gives His beloved sleep.

PSALM 127:1–2

PSALM 127 IS WRITTEN BY SOLOMON. HE
writes about the blessed life of the righteous, pointing
out that a life without the blessing of the Lord is futile.
We cannot build anything that will stand unless the Lord
blesses it. It doesn't matter how hard we work, how late
we stay up, how early we rise, or how many hours we put
in, if the Lord does not choose to bless those hours. It is

vanity for us to chase after something wholeheartedly if we have not first sought after the Lord. The second half of the psalm points out that children are a blessing from the Lord, but just as any work cannot be prosperous unless the Lord's blessing is on it, your childrearing will not be fruitful unless the Lord is in it.

In Matthew 6:33, Jesus says, "But seek first the kingdom of God and His righteousness, and all these things shall be added to you." This comes on the heels of His exhortation against worry. When God is first in our lives, we won't have to worry about having food, houses, money, and any other necessity. God will fill in all the gaps. When we keep our eyes on Him, committing our ways to Him, then our work will prosper.

The patience that Solomon is calling for in Psalm 127 is a sharp contrast to our get-ahead-first, take-every-opportunity, hustle culture. In most professional environments, the most aggressive people will be the most successful. Solomon says hard work is good, but we must seek the Lord in our work. He says to build, but to ask the Lord to build with us. He says to have children, but to commit them to the Lord. He is calling for a patience that isn't trying to get ahead of God's timing.

In 2013, *The Atlantic* published a blog post entitled "How America's 'Culture of Hustling' Is Dark and Empty,"* in which the author sought to answer the ques-

---

* David Masciotra, *The Atlantic*, April 13, 2013, https://www.the-atlantic.com/health/archive/2013/08/how-americas-culture-of-hustling-is-dark-and-empty/278601/.

tion: How do you differentiate between pointless hustling and meaningful work? The article's conclusion was, "If you are open to it, courage will find you; you don't have to go looking for it (which I don't think will work anyway). What was that line from Augustine? 'Love God and do what thou wilt.' For 'God' I substitute 'Truth.'"

They really didn't need any substitution. God is the truth they are seeking. And yes, if they seek God, they will find that all other things are added to them. They will find that there is no reason to hustle furiously because He is the One who brings prosperity.

Understanding that the Lord is the One who prospers our work brings peace in the fear of missing out on opportunities. There is never a reason to sacrifice obedience for seeking after an opportunity. If we are failing to love our children so that we can take a promotion, our work will not be prosperous. If we are failing to show hospitality, or skimping on our church attendance, or failing to show generosity, or hiding our faith from unbelievers, we are not seeking God's kingdom first. Anything we pursue while we are ignoring obedience will not be blessed. But God will pour out His blessings at the perfect time, and our job is to seek Him first. If we seek His kingdom by obeying Him, then He will bless our efforts and bring us increase in His own way and in His own time. We should not strive for greatness. We have to wait for God to build the house.

Consider ways you might have aggressively pursued a goal at the cost of obedience to God. Turn your pursuits toward God in patience by reminding yourself of this truth: "Unless You build the house, I labor in vain."

GOD'S PROMISE
TO HEAR US

The righteous cry out, and the LORD hears,
and delivers them out of all their troubles.
The LORD is near to those who have a broken heart,
and saves such as have a contrite spirit.

PSALM 34:17–18

GOD IS LISTENING. HE IS LISTENING WHEN
we ask Him for financial provision, He is listening when
we ask Him for healing, He is listening when we ask Him
for the salvation of a loved one. He hears the righteous
every time we talk to Him, He considers all of our requests, and then He sends deliverance.

David wrote Psalm 34 after he pretended to be insane so that Abimelech would not consider him a
threat. He does not take the credit for the idea to act cra-
zy. He praises God, saying that God was the One who

delivered Him. Even in situations where something or someone helps us when we are in trouble, we need to recognize that they are God's tools for deliverance. God can use counselors to deliver us from depression, doctors to deliver us from illness, or parents to deliver us from financial crisis. Sometimes our troubles are nothing more than a toddler with a defiant attitude and a newborn baby who doesn't sleep. He uses so many tangible means to deliver us. Cry out to Him for a night of good sleep and for wisdom to stick to a schedule. Maybe He will deliver you by sending your mother-in-law for an afternoon. Sometimes we feel stuck in a dead-end job and have received no callbacks from the hundreds of applications sent out. Deliverance will come. God is always planning ways to set us free. David says that the Lord delivers the humble from *all* their troubles. He delivers from heavy trials like infertility, and He delivers from minuscule trials like a headache.

If you don't already keep a prayer journal, it can be extremely helpful to write down the situations you are asking the Lord to deliver you from. This allows you to look back over all the ways that He has answered your cries. If He hasn't answered your prayer, then He hasn't finished that part of your story. Deliverance comes. Sometimes it takes ten or twenty years, sometimes ten or twenty minutes, but it always comes. Keep reminding yourself of all the ways He has rescued you in the past, and your faith for the struggles remaining will be strong. Sometimes deliverance looks different than we think it should. But if you believe God is the Deliverer, you will see the deliverance in whatever form it comes.

In verse 4, David says that God delivered him from all his *fears*. Fear of the future can create a tougher trial than actually walking through the trial itself. Fear itself is a horrific burden, even if the fear never comes to fruition. When we allow ourselves to be gripped by real or imagined fears, it paralyzes us spiritually. But even fear, the trial that is often just our false imagination of the future, gets God's attention and He delivers us. He is kind and compassionate. He tells us often not to fear, but when we fail, He sets us free.

A couple of years ago, my oldest daughter started attending school for the first time. She was excited, but as the first day of school approached, she became nervous and fearful. "What if the teacher is mean?" she would ask. "What if none of the kids like me and I don't have friends? What if I can't remember all the things I'm supposed to learn?" We would read Psalm 34, and I told her three things: "First, God hears you when you ask Him for a kind teacher and friends and a sharp memory. Second, if something bad happens, God will send a way to deliver you from it. Third, God will also deliver you from being afraid. He will send you courage." Explaining this psalm to a child gave me a new perspective on the power of this promise. And it gave fresh content to my prayers for her.

Verse 20 is a prophecy about Jesus. It says, "He guards all his bones, not one of them is broken." This is foretelling the time when Jesus was on the cross and the soldiers, seeing He was already dead, decided not to break His legs to speed up the suffocation process. We are again connected with Christ as we pray this psalm. As we praise God for all the deliverance He has sent us in the past and re-establish our hope of deliverance in the future, we can rest assured that He will show us the same care that He showed to His own Son. Even in Christ's darkest moment, the Father kept His promises to Him.

Are you in trouble? Are you afraid of trouble? Pray for deliverance and find hope by preaching this truth to yourself: "The righteous cry out, and the LORD hears, and delivers them out of all their troubles."

GOD'S FORGIVENESS

When I kept silent, my bones grew old
through my groaning all the day long.
For day and night Your hand was heavy upon me;
My vitality was turned into the drought of summer. *Selah*
I acknowledged my sin to You
and my iniquity I have not hidden.
I said, "I will confess my transgressions to the LORD,"
and You forgave the iniquity of my sin. *Selah*
For this cause everyone who is godly shall pray to You
in a time when You may be found;
surely in a flood of great waters
they shall not come near him.
You are my hiding place;
You shall preserve me from trouble;
You shall surround me with songs of deliverance. *Selah*

PSALM 32:3–7

SOMETIMES WHEN WE GO TO GOD IN PRAYER
it seems like He is not listening. We can feel like the

weight isn't lifted, or like He is moving to action very quickly. One of the first places to start when this happens is to make sure we have confessed our own sin. As David says in Psalm 32, when he kept silent, his bones grew old through groaning. Holding onto sin even affects our physical health. We become confused, overwhelmed, and stressed out. But when we confess our sin to God, He forgives us for our petty annoyances, for our self-pity, for our laziness, for our lack of self-control, for our lack of faith and hope, for believing that He isn't good, for unkindness to children, for shortness with spouses, for disrespect of parents, and we are restored. David says that God is quick to forgive. And what does David find in the forgiveness? He finds protection and he finds song. He does not want to lose the fellowship that he has with God, which protects him from falling into sin again.

I have sought to reflect this aspect of our relationship with God in my own family. After we correct our children, we instruct them to ask for forgiveness from anyone they have sinned against. Forgiveness must be genuinely extended. But what then? The goal is to be back in fellowship with everyone in the family and be cheerful. Sometimes I have noticed that this last step is difficult. It is hard for them to turn from the point of confessing a sin to the point of feeling safe and happy and restored. It is important that I don't just let my children hide themselves in their room to wallow in self-pity after they have been disciplined. When I look at things from their perspective, I need to make sure that coming

back into fellowship with the family is something that
is appealing. Does restoration to fellowship mean that
they have to come sit down at the table with a grumpy
and tired mom? Does restoration to fellowship mean
they have to continue playing with a sibling who was
provoking them?

Restoration to fellowship should be something that
my children look forward to, something that they want,
something that is so good it will be a protection around
them. If I am grumpy, why would they want to be around
me? If I am cheerful and kind, if I am filling our home
with good food and creative toys and fun movie nights
and music, then they will want to be part of it. They can
see that their sin creates a breach between them and having a joyful time, and they will be eager to turn from their
sin so that they can jump right back into the family. Any
time one of my children is stuck in a pattern of sinning in
a certain way, I look to make sure that I have created an at-
mosphere of joyful fellowship that they want to be in. This
can go a long way to motivate them towards obedience.

If I am not fully forgiving my children, then I am creating a breach of fellowship. My children know if I am
defining them by their sin. They know when I consider
them the "hyper" child or the "emotional" child. Why
would they want to come back into fellowship with
someone who considers them too emotional? David's
comfort and joy in Psalm 32 comes because of the deep
assurance that his sin is completely forgotten. In order
to restore my relationship with my children, I need to

completely forget about their sin. I cannot talk about their sin to others; I cannot bring it up if they sin again; I cannot let them wear that sin.

I can only show this kind of full forgiveness to my family if I believe that God has shown it to me. If I am forgiven, then I will forgive. I cannot keep silent about my own sin. I need to confess and acknowledge it before God. If I fail to seek forgiveness, then I fail to forgive. If I fail to forgive, then I fail to protect from further sin. Do you see how we are like children before God? Our sin causes a breach in our fellowship with Him, but when we are forgiven, we can be restored into His joy. Psalm 16:11 says, "In Your presence is fullness of joy; at Your right hand there are pleasures forevermore." Even while we live in our bodies, we know that being in fellowship with God means fullness of joy. But we cannot find that joy if we are not accepting His full forgiveness. If we wear our sin, if we define our lives by our sin, if we try to cling to any part of it, we are not letting forgiveness in Christ define our identity. His forgiveness is our protection and our gateway into His presence.

Confess your sin to the Lord. Thank Him for His forgiveness, which protects you and gives you strength to forgive. Remind yourself of the fellowship you have with God through forgiveness with these words: "You are my hiding place; You shall preserve me from trouble; You shall surround me with songs of deliverance."

GOD'S REWARD

Light is sown for the righteous,
and gladness for the upright in heart.
PSALM 97:11

PSALM 97 IS A PRAISE TO THE LORD FOR His power and His righteousness. The psalmist declares how the whole world brings glory to God, and how those who do not acknowledge Him will be destroyed. But for the righteous, God has sown light and gladness. His plan is to give joy to the obedient.

I remember feeling offended when I was disciplined as a child. To me the infliction of pain did not seem like the most effective way to get me to stop doing something. My parents would reassure me that they were doing this for my good. I would often feel confused because goodness and pain were disconnected in my mind. How could something bring me good if it is painful? Obviously, I had a lot to learn at the age of five.

I have continued to find that obedience is often painful, and that gladness doesn't always come immediately. That is why we have to keep this promise in Psalm 97 in the forefront of our minds. God says that He is sowing light for the righteous, and gladness for the upright. If you are upright, obeying His commands, then joy is coming to you even if it feels painful to obey in the present.

There are many times when obedience is painful. It is painful to obey authorities who are asking us to do things that we do not want to do. It is painful to deny our own desires for the sake of obedience. It is painful to discipline your own children. It is painful to confront a friend who is in sin. It is painful to risk your friendship for the sake of righteousness. It is painful to care for loved ones who are ill. Generosity and hospitality can be painful if our resources are already stretched thin. All these things are obedience to God, but they can hurt. The gladness that is promised from obedience is not immediate in many circumstances, which is why we must have faith that God will give what He has promised. When the widow gave her two mites, Jesus loved her gift even more than the much larger gifts of the Pharisees. He knew that her gift was all she had. Her generosity had the potential to cause her great discomfort in the future, but she still obeyed. Our biggest sacrifices in our lives will feel painful. If they did not, they would not be sacrifices. In our obedience, we have hope. Obedience always brings joy in the end.

When we are looking at troubling circumstances facing us, it can be easy to see the discomfort. Do not focus on the pain. Do not think about how much of yourself you will have to give. Focus on how you can obey. Do not dwell on what will make you the happiest immediately. Choose your course of action based on what God tells you to do. Obedience might feel dark for a time. Discipline is never pleasant. But on the other side, there is light. When God sees obedience, He starts planting for you. He starts preparing a gift of joy.

When obedience to God is painful, preach this hopeful truth to yourself: "Light is sown for the righteous, and gladness for the upright in heart."

WAITING ON GOD

Out of the depths I have cried to You, O LORD;
Lord, hear my voice!
Let Your ears be attentive
to the voice of my supplications.
If You, LORD, should mark iniquities,
O Lord, who could stand?
But there is forgiveness with You,
that You may be feared.
I wait for the LORD, my soul waits,
and in His word I do hope.

PSALM 130:1–5

IN PSALM 130, WE SEE THE WRITER RESTING in the waiting. He says he is in the depths, but he believes that the Lord will hear him even in his darkest times. He acknowledges that if the Lord had kept track of his sin, then he would never be delivered. He knows he has sinned, but he also knows he is forgiven. Because he has assurance of his forgiveness, he can find hope in crying out to God. After his cry, he tells the Lord that he will wait and hope. He will wait because he knows God is listening, and he will hope because he knows God's Word. He knows what God is like, and from His Word the writer knows God to be a listener and a deliverer.

Whenever we are struggling, when we need God to come to our rescue, when circumstances are overwhelmingly hard, we need to take note from this psalm and look for things that get in the way of our hope for deliverance. First, we need to understand that we are totally forgiven of all our sins. God is not punishing us by withholding answers. If we have confessed our sins and turned from them, then we can rest assured that our trial is not punishment. As the psalmist notes, if God was keeping track of our failures, then none of us could stand for a second. Our trials are not a sign that God doesn't love us or that He hasn't forgiven us. Our trials are His refining tool to sanctify us.

Another thing that can block our hearts from hope is not knowing His Word. The psalmist says that in the Word he finds hope. God's Word is full of stories of deliverance: Noah from the flood, Joseph from prison, Moses from Pharaoh's death sentence, the Israelites from Egypt, Abraham and Sarah from barrenness. The Old Testament is a series of stories all about God listening to the cry of His people and delivering them from their trials. When we know His Word, we find hope. When we study His Word, we feed our hope and we can patiently

continue to plead with Him in our troubles, because we
know Him to be attentive.

In verse 5, the writer of this psalm says that he will
wait on the Lord. I think this is the hardest part of a
trial. If we knew going into an illness how long it would
last, then it would be easier to endure because we would
have a date of deliverance to look forward to. If we knew
at what point our challenging child would mature, it
would be easier to have patience with them during the
waiting. But many trials have indefinite waiting. Culti-
vating endurance is extremely important for Christians,
and waiting on the Lord gives us the opportunity to do
that. We can turn to His Word to give us the fuel we
need for endurance, memorizing it, and reminding our
hearts constantly of the hope we have in Him.

2 Peter 1:3 says, "As His divine power has given to us
all things that pertain to life and godliness, through the
knowledge of Him who called us by glory and virtue."
This means we already have everything we need to live
a life of godliness. While we wait for God to answer our
prayers, we are not waiting to become godly. We have
everything we need to endure trials. If we struggle with
depression, He has offered us everything we need to endure the dark days. If we struggle through grief and loss,
we have everything we need to endure the loneliness. If
we struggle with sins like anger or impatience or envy
or complaining, God has offered everything we need to
overcome the enemy. So as we wait on Him to deliver us
completely, we can find hope and patience in knowing

that we have everything we need to live a godly life in the middle of hardship.

Philippians 4:13 gives us additional fuel, "I can do all things through Christ who strengthens me." If we are going to cultivate endurance, then we must remind ourselves of this daily, sometimes hourly. We can endure! We can wait! We can hope! Because Christ will strengthen us to do all things. He will strengthen us to face the hard days, and He will strengthen us to face the boring days where the sin of self-pity taps at the door like an old friend. He will strengthen us like an IV strengthens a sick patient. He will be infusing us with His power so that we can endure all the waiting until the Lord comes with full deliverance to lift us out of the pit.

As you wait for the Lord to deliver you from your struggles, preach this truth to yourself: "I wait for the LORD, my soul waits, and in His word I do hope." You can find rest in the waiting if you seek to find your strength in Christ.

CONCLUSION

He heals the brokenhearted
and binds up their wounds. . .
He does not delight in the strength of the horse;
He takes no pleasure in the legs of a man.
The LORD takes pleasure in those who fear Him,
in those who hope in His mercy.

PSALM 147:3, 10–11

JESUS SAID THAT IN THIS WORLD WE WILL
have trouble (Jn. 16:33). Not one of us can go through
this life without experiencing some kind of pain. Some
of us will have more pain than others, but at some point
all of our hearts will be hurt because this world is full of
sin, and pain is the fruit of sin. Jesus goes on to say that
we should not be afraid of this painful world because
He has overcome it. God has come as man incarnate to
bind up wounds, to heal broken hearts. God is carefully

213

working in your story to make your heart and mind whole. In our culture, we love to talk about trauma. We love to dig deep into someone's story and find what may have caused them to be depressed or discontent or self-ish or angry. God knows all of our stories better than we do. He can see exactly what happened, and He knows the right pathway for healing.

In verses 10–11 of Psalm 147, the author says that God does not delight in the strength of a horse or the legs of a man. God does not want us to put our trust in the things of this world that seem strong. He does not want us to put our faith in doctors or counselors or med-ication or organic food. He takes pleasure in those who fear Him and hope in His mercy. He wants us to look to Him to heal our brokenness. He wants us to have faith that He is the One who binds up our wounds. The Lord certainly can use the materials of this world, and espe-cially other wise people, to help us heal and overcome sin. But He does not want our faith to be in them. He wants us to see them as tools for victory, not as saviors. He wants us to praise Him for the helpful counseling we have received, but He does not want us to see the coun-selor as the Healer. If we have been walking through a trial for a long time and our hearts are feeling shattered and broken, it is natural to think that if we could just find the right advice or counsel or physician or diet, then we would be able to break free and move on from our pain. But this is not where we will find answers. We can pray for God to guide us to a counselor or a doctor that would help us gain victory over our trial. We can actively search for solutions if we view them as tools from God. Even then we need to be praying, "Lord, *You* are the One who heals brokenness. Guide me to someone who can help me heal. Show me the path I should take. I trust *You* to bind up my wounds with whatever means You choose." He is merciful. He does listen. He will guide us.

As you read through the Psalms, mark passages that encourage you. Write them down, memorize them, sing them, carry them in your pocket, meditate on them when you have a quiet moment. When you pray, use the passages as a guide for your words. Whether you are pleading with God through a difficult trial, or just asking for strength in your everyday work, the Psalms will teach you how to approach God and what to ask for. When you go about your daily tasks, use the Psalms of praise to give your heart words of gratitude. Let the Psalms shape your perspective of God's character. Let them teach you about His care and love for you. When you are discouraged and losing hope, read the Psalms. Find the truth of God's grace and preach it to your heart. Feed your soul with the Psalms. They are tools for building your faith.

The Book of Psalms is a great gift to us as we seek to understand how to walk through life. They show us what God is like, how He wants us to think and live, and how we should talk to Him. The Psalms help us to understand what our relationship with God should look like. We can learn about His character and about what He wants from us. We learn how to fear God in the Psalms. In psalm 147 we learn that He takes pleasure in those who fear Him and those who hope in His mercy. When we use these words in our prayers, we learn what it looks like to hope in His mercy. The Psalms give us guidance in life and words to pray. They give us strong defenses in our minds against all kinds of sin. David teaches us to learn God's character by looking at what He has done through all of history, and by looking at what He has done for us specifically. Remembering God's acts of goodness provides our hearts and minds with a wall of defense. In the war to love God with all our hearts, with all our souls, and with all our minds, *remembering* is our greatest weapon. The Book of Psalms is our prayer book to give us this strength, just as it was the prayer book of David and of Jesus. The Psalms are for trials. The Psalms are for us.